The Church with AIDS

Also published by The Westminster Press

Books by Letty M. Russell

Household of Freedom: Authority in Feminist
    Theology
Becoming Human (*Library of Living Faith* series)
Growth in Partnership
The Future of Partnership
Human Liberation in a Feminist Perspective—
    A Theology
Christian Education in Mission

Other books edited by Letty M. Russell

Inheriting Our Mothers' Gardens: Feminist Theology
    in Third World Perspective (with Kwok Pui-lan,
    Ada María Isasi-Díaz, and Katie Geneva Cannon)
Feminist Interpretation of the Bible
The Liberating Word: A Guide to Nonsexist Interpre-
    tation of the Bible

The Church with AIDS

Renewal in the Midst of Crisis

Letty M. Russell, editor

Westminster/John Knox Press
Louisville, Kentucky

Scripture quotations from the Revised Standard Version of the Bible are copyrighted 1946, 1952, © 1971, 1973 by the Division of Christian Education of the National Council of the Churches of Christ in the U.S.A., and are used by permission. Scripture quotations marked * are from *An Inclusive-Language Lectionary, Year A*, revised edition, © 1986; *Year B*, revised edition, © 1987; and *Year C*, revised edition, © 1988 by the Division of Education and Ministry of the National Council of the Churches of Christ in the U.S.A., and are used by permission. The scripture quotation in chapter 1 marked NIV is from *The Holy Bible, New International Version.* Copyright © 1973, 1978, 1984 International Bible Society. Used by permission of Zondervan Bible Publishers.

Design and engraving of "We Are the Church Alive" is copyright © 1989, The Hymnal Project, 150 Eureka Street, San Francisco, CA 94114. Reprinted by permission.

Dedicated to Ron Russell-Coons, with thanks for the gift of life he shared with us.

First edition

Published by Westminster/John Knox Press
Louisville, Kentucky

PRINTED IN THE UNITED STATES OF AMERICA

9   8   7   6   5   4   3   2   1

Library of Congress Cataloging-in-Publication Data

The Church with AIDS : renewal in the midst of crisis / Letty M. Russell, editor. — 1st ed.
    p.   cm.
Includes bibliographical references.
ISBN 0-664-25111-0

  1. AIDS (Disease)—Patients—Pastoral counseling of. 2. AIDS (Disease)—Religious aspects—Christianity. 3. AIDS phobia. 4. Church work with gays. I. Russell, Letty M.
BV4460.7.C468 1990
261.8′321969792—dc20   90-32432

Contents

Preface

What happens when a group of Christians comes together over the course of five years to reflect on the nature of the church in light of struggles for justice, and on the nature of those struggles in the light of our understanding of the church? This book is one answer to those questions.

Such a group has been meeting as part of the Commission on Faith and Order of the National Council of the Churches of Christ in the U.S.A., hereafter referred to as the National Council of Churches. The commission gathers for three days twice a year and provides an opportunity for representatives of some forty Protestant, Roman Catholic, and Orthodox denominations to work together on theological issues affecting our common life. The work of the commission is carried out in study groups. In recent years different study groups have focused on issues of how denominations respond to each other's doctrines and ministries, on the meaning of creeds as part of apostolic faith, and, more recently, on the ecumenical writing of church history and on the work of the Holy Spirit and the church.

Starting in the spring of 1985, the study group that had previously focused on developing an understanding of contextual theology undertook to respond to an initiative of the World Council of Churches' Faith and Order Commission made through a study document titled "The Unity of the Church and the Renewal of Human Community."[1] The issue described had to do with attempting to discern connections between the unity of the church—usually assumed to be the business of doctrinal discussions—and the renewal going on in local communities, regions, and countries—usually assumed to be the focus of mission work. The World Council effort focused on understanding possible connections across traditional lines of doctrine and mission and thereby exploring the interdependence of the unity of the church and the struggles for justice in the world.

Therefore, the Study Group on the Unity of the Church and the Renewal of Human Community of the National Council of Churches' Commission on Faith and Order adopted as its purpose "to reflect theologically with groups engaged in human renewal to discover how understanding of the unity and mission of the church shifts in such contexts of struggle for life."[2] The particular focus of our investigations was to be points where a theology of life is emerging from situations of struggle and where ecclesiology, or our understanding of the church, is changing in response to situations of struggle and death.

The study group decided to do initial case studies with "groups engaged in human renewal" in which at least one study group member was a participant. This led to case study presentations on AIDS, on plant closings and economic justice, on church professional development, on the changing roles of men and women at the parish level, and on liberation struggles in Latin America. Following the case studies, the study group looked for "ecclesiological clues": What insights did the case studies provide into how people engaged in "struggles for life" understood the nature of the church? What did our group see as a result of reflection on those connections?[3]

The study group used what has been described as the "spiral model" of theological reflection: that is, we engaged in Bible study, action (through the action of the case study groups), reflection, and a search for ecclesiological clues. The spiral may be started from any of these points. It may be continued for several rounds by, for example, following up new clues with further Bible study, action through case studies, and reflection, and yet further clues.

The particular focus on AIDS represented by this book has its origin in the case study presented to the study group in 1986 by Metropolitan Community Church (MCC) liaisons Jennie Boyd Bull and Janet Pierce. Further contributions were made by Ron Russell-Coons, a person living with AIDS who joined the study group in 1988. Because we focused on AIDS, using the experience of our MCC members as the point of entry, the bulk of our material for reflection centered on the experience of gay, white males living with AIDS. This was, therefore, our primary base for seeking clues from which to develop an understanding of the church in light of the AIDS crisis. If we had decided to engage in another round in the spiral of theological reflection, other aspects of the church's encounter with AIDS could have been explored. That the impact of AIDS among blacks, Latinos, women, and I.V. drug users, for example, and the spread of the disease among heterosexuals and society are generally in the background of our discussion is not because we think those issues are of secondary importance. Essentially, we have completed one round of the spiral. This is both the achievement and the limitation of this particular book.

We have all seen books that are collections of papers by people who have not worked together and that reflect the limited nature of the collaboration. This work, through its collection of essays, is intentionally more integrated. This is not to say all of us agreed on all the points of view developed here. But the discussion and critique of each other's work, the sharing of life experiences and gathering as a worshiping community as well as a community of scholars, pastors, and denominational workers, are reflected in the following pages. This book attempts to exemplify in a useful and exciting way how people working together over a period of time can enrich and build on each other's work.

As cochairs we wish to express our appreciation to all the members of the study group for their faithful work, and particularly to Letty Russell for undertaking the role of editor. We give special thanks for the presence and efforts of Ron Russell-Coons. His willingness to devote so much energy to the development of this book at a time when his own struggle with AIDS so greatly taxes his strength is an example of generosity and grace for which we are all deeply grateful.

The spiral method of theological reflection is limited only to the extent that there are time and workers in the vineyard to carry out new rounds! We welcome you, the readers, as new participants in this venture.

RANDALL C. BAILEY AND ANNE P. SCHEIBNER
Cochairs, Study Group on Unity and Renewal,
Commission on Faith and Order,
National Council of the Churches
of Christ in the U.S.A.

Acknowledgments

Acknowledgment is made to the following for use of material in chapter 10, "Life Stories":

"David's Story," "Carole's Story," and "No Name" are used with permission of the author, Ron Russell-Coons.

"Hector's Story: AIDS and the Church in Puerto Rico" is used with permission of the author, L'Anni Hill-Alto, a Reformed Church in America pastor in Puerto Rico.

"Our Babies" is used with permission of the author, J. Tamshel (a pseudonym used to protect the identity of the children).

"Jane's Story: The Scarlet A" is used with permission of the author, the Reverend R. Page Fulgham, pastor of the First Baptist Church of Lawrenceville, Georgia.

"Carl's Story: Moved to Act" is used with permission of the authors, the Reverends James O. Gilliom and Faith V. Ferre, pastors of the Plymouth Congregational United Church of Christ in Des Moines, Iowa.

"Chuck's Story: The First Iconium Baptist Church" is used with permission of the author, the Reverend Timothy McDonald, pastor of the First Iconium Baptist Church in Atlanta.

"The Hidden Grievers: AIDS-Related Bereavement" is used with permission of the author, Patrick Cogan, SA.

Acknowledgment is made to *The Christian Century* for the use of material in chapter 11, first published as an article titled "We Are the Church Alive, the Church with AIDS" (issue of January 27, 1988).

Acknowledgment is made to the following persons and organizations for use of material in chapter 13, "Resources for Study and Action":

The Southern Baptist Churches' statement in response to AIDS is used with permission of the author, the Reverend R. Page Fulgham.

The "Theological Statement Developed by the Union of Black Episcopalians' AIDS Task Force" is used with permission of the Union of Black Episcopalians (UBE). For additional information on the Union of Black Episcopalians' AIDS Task Force (UBEAT), contact the Rev. Charles L. Poindexter, UBEAT Convener, St. Luke's Episcopal Church, 5421 Germantown Avenue, Philadelphia, PA 19144, or the Rev. Dr. Mwalimu Imara, Morehouse Medical School, Atlanta, GA 30310.

The Universal Fellowship of Metropolitan Community Churches' statement in response to AIDS is used with permission of the author, the Reverend Jennie Boyd Bull, who is a pastor in a UFMCC church, and is based on an article first printed in *Journey*, UFMCC/Los Angeles, Pentecost 1987.

The "Liturgy for Casting Out Fear" was developed by a committee chaired by Arthur Freeman at the Moravian Theological Seminary, and is used with permission. The poem "The Face of AIDS," found in the Confession in Unison, is reprinted from *A Shallow Pool of Time: An HIV+ Woman Grapples with the AIDS Epidemic*, by permission of New Society Publishers (Philadelphia, Pa., and Santa Cruz, Calif.).

The "Liturgy for Casting Out Stones" was developed by the Religious Coalition on AIDS, Bethlehem, Pennsylvania, and is used with permission of its principal author, Earl D. Ball.

The "Litany of Healing" was written by the Reverend Traci West for an ecumenical service of healing and prayer given in Hartford, Connecticut, on December 12, 1989, and is used with permission.

The hymn "We Are the Church Alive," with text by the Rev. Jack Hoggatt-St. John and the Rev. David Pelletier and music by Jack Hoggatt-St. John, is taken from *The Hymnal Project* (San Francisco: Metropolitan Community Church, 1989), and is used and reproduced with permission.

Contributors

RANDALL C. BAILEY is Assistant Professor of Old Testament and Hebrew at the Interdenominational Theological Center in Atlanta. He is an ordained Baptist minister. He is the author of *David in Love and War: The Pursuit of Power in 2 Samuel 10–12*, and of several articles on the Old Testament and ancient Africa. He is cochair of the Study Group on Unity and Renewal of the Commission on Faith and Order of the National Council of Churches, and is the first African-American to serve on the Bible Translation and Utilization Committee of the NCC.

KITTREDGE CHERRY became a Metropolitan Community Church minister in 1989, and joined the staff of the Metropolitan Community Church of San Francisco while a seminarian. She is also a professional writer whose articles have appeared in such publications as *The Wall Street Journal* and *Newsweek*. A graduate of the University of Iowa, she lived in Japan for three years before moving to San Francisco with her spouse, Audrey E. Lockwood. She is the author of *Womansword: What Japanese Words Say About Women*, and a forthcoming book about secrets and spirituality. She cowrote the article "We Are the Church Alive, the

Church with AIDS" while a student at the Pacific School of Religion in Berkeley, California.

J. SHANNON CLARKSON is Special Lecturer at the University of New Haven and Staff Consultant for the Division of Education and Ministry of the National Council of Churches. She was ordained to the ministry in 1978 and served as copastor of the First Congregational Church of West Haven for ten years. Her doctoral thesis was on the contributions of inclusive language to the educational ministry of the church, and she is the author of a recently published National Council of Churches booklet titled "Language, Thought, and Social Justice." She is active in the Commission on Faith and Order of the National Council of Churches and is cochair of the Bible Translation and Utilization Committee of the NCC.

PATRICK COGAN, SA, is the editor of *Ecumenical Trends* and associate director of the Graymoor Ecumenical Institute, New York. He holds graduate degrees from The Catholic University of America, Washington, D.C., and St. Paul University, Ottawa, Ontario. He is also a member of the Franciscan Friars of the Atonement, a Roman Catholic religious community dedicated to Christian unity.

SUSAN E. DAVIES is Associate Professor of Pastoral Studies at Bangor Theological Seminary, Bangor, Maine. She is ordained in the United Church of Christ and has served parishes in Maine, Connecticut, and California.

ARTHUR J. FREEMAN is Professor of Biblical Theology, New Testament, Moravian Theological Seminary, Bethlehem, Pennsylvania, where he also teaches spiritual formation and administers the continuing education program. He received his Ph.D. from Princeton Theological Seminary, Princeton, New Jersey, and serves on the Faith and Order Commissions of both the National Council of Churches and the Moravian Church in America.

JOHN is in the process of seeking ordination and looking for a job; therefore he has decided not to use his full name. His sexual orientation, about which he is fairly open, may well prevent him from being hired by a parish. If his HIV status were made known, it is virtually certain he would be regarded as unemployable even by the most "liberal" of churches. In another situation, he might be inclined to make an issue of it, but he needs a church job and the insurance coverage too much to take that risk.

BERYL INGRAM-WARD is the pastor of St. Paul's United Methodist Church, Tacoma, Washington. She was a member of the hymnal revision committee that produced the United Methodist Church hymnal of 1989, and in that process was an advocate for inclusive language and for fresh images for the deity. She and her husband, Bob, are a United Methodist Church clergy couple and live in Auburn, Washington.

JAMES MITULSKI has been pastor of the Metropolitan Community Church of San Francisco for four years. For the three years before that, he was assistant pastor of the Metropolitan Community Church in New York City, where he first encountered AIDS. He is a graduate of Columbia University and cowrote the article "We Are the Church Alive, the Church with AIDS" while a student at the Pacific School of Religion, Berkeley,

California. He lives with his lover Bob Crocker, whom he met in college in 1977.

LETTY M. RUSSELL is Professor of Theology at Yale Divinity School, New Haven, Connecticut. She was ordained to the ministry in 1958 by the United Presbyterian Church U.S.A., and served as a pastor and educator in the East Harlem Protestant Parish for seventeen years. She is the author of *Household of Freedom: Authority in Feminist Theology*, and the editor of *Feminist Interpretation of the Bible* and *Inheriting Our Mothers' Gardens: Feminist Theology in Third World Perspective*. She is active in the Commission on Faith and Order of the National Council of Churches and in the World Council of Churches.

RON RUSSELL-COONS is clergy on the staff of the Metropolitan Community Church of San Francisco. He represents the Universal Fellowship of Metropolitan Community Churches on the Faith and Order Commission of the National Council of Churches. A person living with AIDS, Russell-Coons has traveled extensively, sharing a message of renewal and hope.

KATHARINE DOOB SAKENFELD is Professor of Old Testament Literature at Princeton Theological Seminary, Princeton, New Jersey. A Presbyterian minister, she is a member of the National Council of Churches' Commission on Faith and Order and has served on the Women's Task Force of the Consultation on Church Union and on the Revised Standard Version Bible Committee. She has published books and essays on feminist issues and problems in the Hebrew scriptures, including "Feminist Biblical Interpretaton" in *Theology Today*, July 1989.

ANNE P. SCHEIBNER is a freelance organizer and active Episcopal laywoman. She has worked with various church groups, including the Interreligious Economic Crisis Organizing Network, the Urban Bishops Coalition of the Episcopal Church, and the Episcopal Women's Caucus. Most recently she edited the experimental "theme issues" published in 1989 of *Jubilee Journal: Social Concerns and the Episcopal Church,* which included an issue devoted to AIDS. She has served as cochair of the National Council of Churches' Unity and Renewal study group since 1988.

ROBERT J. SCHREITER is Professor of Theology at the Catholic Theological Union in Chicago. He received his doctorate from the University of Nijmegen in the Netherlands. Among his books are *Constructing Local Theologies* and *In Water and in Blood: A Spirituality of Solidarity and Hope.* He is editor of *New Theology Review.* He served as cochair of the National Council of Churches' Unity and Renewal study group from 1985 to 1988.

MARJORIE SUCHOCKI recently moved from her position as Academic Dean at Wesley Theological Seminary to accept an appointment as the Ingraham Professor of Theology at the School of Theology at Claremont, California. She received her doctorate at Claremont Graduate School and is the author of books and articles on feminism, process thought, and Christian theology. Her most recent book is a revised and expanded edition of *God, Christ, Church: A Practical Guide to Process Theology.*

Participants in the Study Group on the Unity of the Church and the Renewal of Human Community

(Commission on Faith and Order, National Council of the Churches of Christ in the U.S.A., 1988–91)

RANDALL C. BAILEY, COCHAIR
Progressive National Baptist Convention

J. SHANNON CLARKSON
United Church of Christ

PATRICK COGAN
Roman Catholic Church

SUSAN E. DAVIES
United Church of Christ

G. DONALD FERREE, JR.
The Episcopal Church

ARTHUR J. FREEMAN
Moravian Church
in America

R. PAGE FULGHAM
Southern Baptist
Convention

JEFFREY GROS, DIRECTOR
Roman Catholic Church

L'ANNI HILL-ALTO
Reformed Church
in America

BARBARA HENNINGES, ADMINISTRATOR
The United Methodist Church

CHING-FEN HSIAO
United Church of Christ

BERYL INGRAM-WARD
The United Methodist Church

GLADYS MOORE
Evangelical Lutheran Church in America

DEBORAH MULLEN
Presbyterian Church
(U.S.A.)

LETTY M. RUSSELL
Presbyterian Church
(U.S.A.)

RON RUSSELL-COONS
Universal Fellowship
of Metropolitan Community
Churches

KATHARINE DOOB
SAKENFELD
Presbyterian Church
(U.S.A.)

ANNE P. SCHEIBNER,
COCHAIR
The Episcopal Church

Letty M. Russell

Introduction

> We know that the whole creation has been groaning in travail together until now; and not only the creation, but we ourselves, who have the first fruits of the Spirit, groan inwardly as we wait for adoption as [children], the redemption of our bodies. For in this hope we [are] saved.
> (Rom. 8:22–24a, alt.)[1]

In the first century of our common era Paul labored to speak the good news in a situation of harsh differences. The Roman Empire was united by force and by law, but great barriers divided Jew and Greek, male and female, slave and free, rich and poor, dominated and dominating, powerful and weak. Writing to the church at Rome, Paul speaks a word of "hope . . . against hope" (Rom. 4:18*). In the midst of suffering and the groaning of creation there is a God whose love can bring life in the midst of death.

The story of our own century is not much different. All around us persons, nations, and creation itself groan with the forces of destruction and death. People die of starvation and from imprisonment, war, and sickness, while economic and political empires dominate and oppress them. Yet the word of hope is still among us—the word of the God of life who in spite of all odds threatens us with resurrection!

23

Writing out of the groaning, suffering, and despair of Guatemala, Julia Esquivel declares that what keeps the people from sleeping is "that they have threatened us with resurrection."[2] The martyrs who have been needlessly sacrificed by ruthless government forces continue to share their strength, courage, and love with those who follow, fearing not death, but life without the hope nourished by the people in struggle.[3]

THREATENED WITH RESURRECTION

Along with crises of suffering in places like Central America, South Africa, the Philippines, and the Middle East is the crisis of AIDS. All over the world people's lives and communities are being plunged into darkness and despair by this death-dealing illness called Acquired Immune Deficiency Syndrome. Although no group is spared this disease, like so many other sources of suffering, it falls disproportionately on the disadvantaged and marginal of society. In the United States, for instance, the largest number of cases is among gay white men. Yet in many African nations it strikes women and children most frequently. And large urban areas are beginning to see increasing numbers of poor women of color and their children infected with AIDS. In New Haven, where I live, 27 percent of the people with AIDS are women, compared to the national average of 9 percent.[4] And one in every 58 pregnant women is infected with HIV (Human Immunodeficiency Virus), the virus that leads to AIDS.[5]

AIDS brings to our society a health crisis of global proportions. It brings fear to every community. It brings that same crisis to every one of our churches, challenging us to live up to our faith. As Susan Davies points out in chapter 6, the church is challenged by "three terrifying realities: death, sexuality, and otherness" [ch. 6, p. 95].[6] These three realities challenge the churches to new ministries in solidarity with persons with AIDS, and also to new possibilities for renewal in the midst of crisis.

THE CHURCH WITH AIDS

Echoed throughout this book is Ron Russell-Coons's declaration: We are the church with AIDS! This affirmation begins with the recognition that PWAs (Persons With AIDS) are found in every sector of our society and every confessional church group. This reality is underlined by the life stories shared in Part Four of this book, as well as in the descriptions found in Part One, "Living with AIDS." Yet it goes much deeper than this, for, as one United Church of Christ pastor says, "We are the body of Christ. If part of us has AIDS, we all have AIDS" [ch. 10, p. 159].

In 1 Corinthians 10:16, Paul speaks of the "bread which we break" as a *koinōnia* (community, participation, partnership) in the body of Christ. Paul uses this metaphor to speak of the risen and glorified body of Christ with which believers are united by the power of the Holy Spirit and with which they will be fully united in the new creation (Rom. 7:4, RSV).[7] Paul also uses this metaphor to speak of the community of Christ's people, or the church. Participation, or *koinōnia*, indicates that Christians have a share in Christ's body, because, in eating and drinking, they express their community and unity in the body of Christ as it is represented through the church, and they are united with Christ's heavenly body by the power of the Spirit. Thus, through time and space, in all ages and places, those who are members of Christ's body are united with one another and with Christ (1 Cor. 12:12–27*). As the theological statement of the Union of Black Episcopalians' AIDS Task Force in chapter 13 says,

We are all related. What affects one part of the body, affects all parts. Just as South Africa is the *kairos* place where the justice of God is being made manifest, so is the AIDS crisis the *kairos* time and place where the love of God is made manifest.

We are all part of the one body of Christ. Whether we have AIDS now, we are all part of a body that includes many persons with AIDS and countless more partners, lovers, parents, children, friends, and fellow workers and worshipers who are sharing in the struggle against fear, rejection, illness, poverty, and death. The affirmation we are the church with AIDS states our solidarity with PWAs as the beginning place for us to share in theological reflection on what it means to be the church in the midst of crisis. Recognizing that God often speaks the good news most powerfully through communities of faith and struggle, we listen, work, and pray that we all may be truly threatened with resurrection as the church with AIDS.

> We are the church Alive,
>   The body must be healed;
> Where strife has bruised and battered us,
>   God's wholeness is revealed.

These words, from a hymn by Jack Hoggatt-St. John and David Pelletier [ch. 13, p. 204], come to us from a church that has been moved to become a church with AIDS [ch. 11, p. 165]. The Metropolitan Community Church of San Francisco (MCC San Francisco) is a predominantly white church in a denomination that ministers to the lesbian and gay community. Its witness, and that of the Universal Fellowship of Metropolitan Community Churches (UFMCC), has been an inspiration for all those who wish to reflect on the ways God is speaking to us in the crisis of AIDS.[8] Its ministers and members have joined us in writing this book and in sharing their experiences of living with AIDS. Since they courageously moved to address issues of sexuality when so many churches refuse even to acknowledge the sexuality of homosexual persons, their courage has been challenged over and over by the homophobia of the churches and surrounding society [ch. 11, p. 165].

The high incidence of AIDS among gay men has drawn them into a second terrifying reality: that of death, and the fear of death, judgment, and condemnation. Working through how to live with AIDS and affirm life here and now as well as after death has been a major contribution made by the gay and lesbian community to all those in the church [ch. 3, p. 61]. In such communities that are by definition other in a homophobic society and church, a new reality of community and healing has been discovered that is offered to all who are willing to share [ch. 12, p. 182]. In many parts of the nation the UFMCC and other denominations have moved together to minister ecumenically, as one community with AIDS [ch. 13, p. 195].[9]

This witness is the basis for much of the theological reflection in this book. Many other life stories and examples of churches responding to the AIDS crisis are included as a basis for action and reflection on the meaning of the church, but the experience of the writing group was particularly shaped by the witness of group members Jennie Boyd Bull, Janet Pierce, and Ron Russell-Coons. Early in our study, Jennie Boyd Bull did a case study of work with persons with AIDS and agreed to make sure that the UFMCC would be represented in the group by a person living with AIDS, who would assist us with our writing project [ch. 13, p. 190]. Ron Russell-Coons began to work with us, and he put us in touch with MCC San Francisco, where he is a member of the clergy staff [ch. 2, p. 45]. As Beryl Ingram-Ward testifies in chapter 4, worship with MCC

San Francisco was a mind-changing experience for several members of our group.

RENEWAL IN THE MIDST OF CRISIS

The unique contribution of this book is that it moves from such experiences of the church with AIDS to reflection on what this particular experience of faith and struggle can teach us about the unity of the church as it responds to Christ's call to share in the renewal of the human community. Growing from five years of ecumenical discussion among members of the Faith and Order Commission of the National Council of Churches, these reflections on the nature of the church and clues to renewal in the midst of crisis are themselves an invitation to persons of many confessions to join at an ecumenical roundtable of action and reflection.

Recognizing the great diversity in theological understanding of such issues of sexuality, death, and otherness found among our own group of writers, we are well aware of the frequent disagreements among those of us who are united in Christ's name. Yet we are convinced that the limits of diversity need to expand as we seek to stand in solidarity with those who suffer. In fact, the very act of solidarity in action and reflection may lead us to new perspectives on who our neighbor really is [ch. 12, p. 179]. As Michael Kinnamon says in *Truth and Community: Diversity and Its Limits in the Ecumenical Movement,* unity that does not include "diverse, liberating, truth-seeking community" is not the unity that churches seek.[10] The test of that unity is not just shared doctrine and mutual recognition, but also shared action on behalf of justice and wholeness for all persons.

The method followed in the Study Group on Unity

and Renewal, and in this book, is a spiral of theological engagement. This method begins in the actual context of the community of faith and struggle, where persons engaged in the struggle with AIDS help the community understand what it means to live with AIDS. Next it analyzes the experience of those struggling with AIDS and what this means for those reflecting on this experience. This in turn leads the group to explore new questions that are raised about traditional understandings of the nature of the church. The final phase of the spiral includes examples and suggestions for further action and reflection, so that both the writers and readers of this book can continue the spiral by going more deeply into the experience of struggle, social and theological analysis, questions about tradition, and actions. In this way the theological reflection is embedded in the actual story of the church with AIDS as it seeks renewal in the midst of crisis.

Using this model of theological engagement has allowed us to share in the life stories of churches and communities with AIDS in such a way that we can also share in the gifts of imagination that they have brought to this struggle for life and healing. As Mary Catherine Bateson and Richard Goldsby say in *Thinking AIDS,*

> If we can use the impetus of AIDS to expand and apply knowledge cooperatively and humanely, we may also learn to control the dangers of the arms race and of world hunger and environmental degradation, for the imagination of AIDS is the imagination of human unity, intimately held in the interdependent web of life.[11]

In Part One the imagination of AIDS is shared through the experience and ministry of those living with AIDS. In chapter 1, Ron Russell-Coons challenges us to shared ecumenical reflection on the affirmation "We have AIDS" in his sermon based on 2 Corinthians

4:16–17. Chapter 2, "Letters to Connie," shares actual letters written to Russell-Coons's sister, edited with the help of Patrick Cogan. Part One is completed with chapter 3, a reflection on the experience of dying and living with AIDS entitled "A Journey Toward Freedom," written by a seminary student named John.

Part Two, "A Church Renewed," presents a series of theological reflections by members of our writing team on what living with AIDS means for the renewal of the church. In chapter 4, Beryl Ingram-Ward reflects on her experience at an ecumenical worship service held at MCC San Francisco and looks at the church as a "Space for Hospitality and Hope." In chapter 5, "Dualism in Christian Tradition," Arthur J. Freeman discusses the problem of dualistic thinking in the Christian tradition and offers insight into the need for wholeness in the way churches understand and interpret scripture. In chapter 6, "Oppression and Resurrection Faith," Susan E. Davies analyzes the structures of oppression that underlie the crisis of AIDS, and challenges the church to live out its resurrection faith in solidarity with those who have AIDS.

Part Three looks critically at the signs of the church, and asks how the traditional marks of the church might be seen differently by those struggling with AIDS. Marjorie Suchocki discusses holiness and a renewed church in chapter 7, and Robert J. Schreiter reevaluates the marks of the church in times of transformation in chapter 8. This section on ecclesiology closes with chapter 9, Letty M. Russell's analysis of what it takes for the church to be a church for troubled waters; a church with AIDS.

Part Four, "The Church with AIDS," is designed by J. Shannon Clarkson to make possible the use of the material in this book in study and discussion groups. The life stories in chapter 10 are collected from a wide variety of congregations and groups and have been edited for use in group discussions. Chapter 11, "We Are the Church Alive," by Kittredge Cherry and James Mitulski, supplements the stories with a description of one church's ministry with AIDS. It also provides a context for understanding the many references to MCC San Francisco in other parts of the book. Chapter 12, "Who Is My Neighbor?", is a rereading by Katharine Sakenfeld of the good Samaritan parable in the light of AIDS, and will be very important for groups struggling with their own faith issues. Chapter 13, "Resources for Study and Action," includes samples of denominational responses, worship materials, and questions for use in group discussions. Clarkson has also included a selected bibliography for those who wish to continue the spiral of theological action and reflection.

Throughout the process of writing this book, we have been painfully aware that so much suffering finally leaves us speechless, without words in our mouths or on paper. Nevertheless, we need to put our solidarity with humankind into practice, using both words and actions. With Adrienne Rich in her poem "Natural Resources," each one of us is challenged to say,

> I have to cast my lot with those
> who age after age, perversely,
>
> with no extraordinary power,
> reconstitute the world.[12]

Joining those who reconstitute the world, and the church as well, is risky business. Yet the threat of resurrection may just be a gift of God to all the churches who seek clues to living so the groaning of creation can in some small way become an ode to joy.

Living with AIDS

We are all living with AIDS, both as a worldwide health crisis and in every community and church. Yet many churches still ignore this reality and practice a conspiracy of silence and rejection. Part One of this book invites the reader to break the silence; to share the physical, social, and spiritual pain of living with AIDS. We all live with AIDS, but we can only learn *how* to live with AIDS from those already learning how to face that reality daily.

We enter the spiral of theological engagement by sharing in the experience and the witness of those living with the AIDS virus. To introduce this experience, the writers of the book invite you to share the powerful witness of Ron Russell-Coons as he preached in 1989 to the writers of this book, members of the National Council of Churches' Commission on Faith and Order, and members of the Metropolitan Community Church of San Francisco (the context of Russell-Coons's sermon is described by Beryl Ingram-Ward in chapter 4). In this sermon, "We Have AIDS," Russell-Coons sets the theme of the book and invites us all to share a journey of resurrection faith that is a gift to each of us and to the church. In the midst of his struggle to live with AIDS, Russell-Coons has found renewal,

for the God who has found him in his suffering is a God
who is to be found in the transforming response to living with AIDS rather than in the search for a cause.

In chapter 2, "Letters to Connie," Russell-Coons
continues to share his spiritual journey with us. Living
with AIDS means that many persons in our churches
write and receive such letters, and probably many
more wish they could write or receive them in the
midst of their despair, anger, rejection, and pain. What
is it like to live with the AIDS virus? How do you respond to family members who reject you? How do you
deal with long hospital stays and the loss of your job?
Ron shares these questions with us so we can walk with
him in the "valley of the shadow of death" (Ps. 23:4).
Perhaps we will catch a glimpse of the goodness and
mercy in God's response that can in turn become our
response as members of the body of Christ living with
AIDS.

Chapter 3, "A Journey Toward Freedom," com-
pletes the first step of our theological spiral, with the
witness of a student named John. John is HIV positive
and has begun the struggle with the AIDS virus, but he
is not left without a "cloud of witnesses" (Heb. 12:1),
such as his friend Archie. By detailing Archie's liberation journey, John helps us see how this spiritual journey is not unlike that of others who have had to face
suffering and death and who have done it with courage
and grace. The gay community, and Archie in particular, have struggled for personal freedom, moved into
action on behalf of others, and faced the reality of
death. And we know from the fact that John cannot
give his name in this written witness that the struggle
is not over. But John is able to share with us a challenge to the church, and the promise of God's love in
that struggle.

1 *Ron Russell-Coons*

We Have AIDS

I hope that tonight* you feel an incredible permission to be really present in this moment, perhaps in a way you never have been in a worship service before. Tonight you have permission to feel all of your feelings; to love and be loved; to hug and be hugged; to pray and to be prayed for; to weep and to laugh; to experience the presence of our God in this place. Please pray with me.

Compassionate God, hold us as a mother holds her young. Protect us in our time of searching, seeking, yearning, and longing for answers. Grant unto us a sense of our unity. Free us from our fears and let us know tonight that you alone are our peace. In Christ's name we pray. Amen.

RENEWED DAY BY DAY

I believe that in this moment tonight we are the body of Christ. Through God's enabling Spirit, we have come to this reality. *We have* AIDS. I know that my context is quite different from St. Paul's, but in my own journey

*This sermon was delivered at an ecumenical service at the Metropolitan Community Church of San Francisco, March 10, 1989. The text for that evening was 2 Corinthians 3:17–18; 4:16–18; Luke 10:25–37.

with AIDS I constantly come back to 2 Corinthians, chapter 4, and Paul's words have new meaning for me. "Therefore, we do not lose heart. Though outwardly we are wasting away, yet inwardly we are being renewed day by day. Our light and momentary troubles are achieving for us an eternal glory that far outweighs them all" (2 Cor. 4:16–17, NIV).

So we fix our eyes on that which is unseen, Paul says, because it's eternal. And I am being renewed, being renewed daily by the courage of my many brothers and sisters who are themselves struggling with AIDS. I am being renewed by the support of people who have made a conscious decision to walk with me through my journey with AIDS. I am being renewed by the willingness of my brothers and sisters to struggle theologically with the crisis of AIDS. I am being renewed by the care of physicians, nurses, and friends who are health-care providers and who have become such an indispensable part of my life. I am being renewed by the trustworthy love of my life partner, Chuck, and the abiding love of my parents, Ruth and Charlie. I am being renewed daily by the abiding presence of God with me in my journey with AIDS.

Occasionally I am tempted to view my faith as akin to "wishing on a star." If I wish hard enough, it might happen: I wish upon a star that my friends were not suffering with AIDS. I wish upon a star that there was no such thing as HIV. I wish upon a star that my friends were not suffering. I wish, I wish—and maybe wishing it will make it so. But the reality is, *we have AIDS.* And the reality is that my faith enables me to journey through AIDS. It is my faith that confronts the reality of AIDS and says, "You can make it!" AIDS is a very grim reality indeed. To wish upon a star will not make AIDS disappear.

Us and Them

The future is not encouraging. It is projected that in the next two years the number of AIDS cases in San Francisco will double, and double again in the following two years. The Centers for Disease Control and the World Health Organization no longer provide weekly statistical updates on new cases and the cumulative total of AIDS cases. They simply cannot keep up with the rapidly expanding data. The World Health Organization has said that their published statistics do not accurately reflect the real crisis. For example, many African countries are frequently two to four years behind in their reporting. Health-care systems are overwhelmed. Many victims are threatened with financial ruin. Churches and schools are encountering challenges that divide and alienate. The real victims are on all levels. *We have AIDS.*

Unfortunately, in the midst of this epidemic, agents of alienation and division surround us. There are individuals, communities, and even churches who have hardened their hearts and wave high the banner of "us and them." Their speeches and placards violently scream such frightening statements as, "We don't want a hospice in our neighborhood for persons with AIDS," or "I won't send my children to a school with 'them.'"

We also encounter members of our churches who still regard AIDS as strictly a moral issue. Recently, the World Health Organization donated to the African country of Liberia, a country with a very high incidence of heterosexual AIDS cases, half a million dollars' worth of condoms. This assistance was denounced by a church leader, who declared that anyone who used those condoms was immoral. *Us and them.*

There are still people who, despite the tremendous medical and scientific knowledge we now have about

AIDS, remain ignorant about the disease and its transmission. It is yet another signal of painful rejection and
alienation, and occurs even within families. Next week
I will travel to Alabama to visit my family. I feel this
may be my last visit with them. I say that only because
it is just too difficult to arrange all the necessary medical treatments there. I set myself up for this. I have
dreamed, even "wished upon a star," about this trip. I
dreamed and wished I would stay with my parents, see
my sister Connie, my brother Kelly, and my children
Julie and Joey. But, as it turns out, my family has developed an us-and-them attitude. I discovered that some
family members were definitely staying away from me.
At this point I'm not sure whether or not I'll see my
sister, Connie. My brother-in-law's cousin, who is a
nurse, told him that being in the same room with me
could possibly expose the family to infection with AIDS.
I was excited over the recent birth of my grand-niece,
Lauren. I will not get to see her, because I am a part of
them, that body of people who must be set apart. So I
realize that next week when I journey to Alabama I
will see only my parents. I thank God for that opportunity—to sit back and eat Southern food and enjoy their
company and love. But, unfortunately, elsewhere in
my family the us-and-them attitude will prevent my
sharing in their love. AIDS *is our reality.*

Often, as a community, we live on the edge of hysteria. The African experience of AIDS is quite different
from our experience in San Francisco. In Africa, it is
children and women who suffer with AIDS. An anthro-
pological model for communities states that in every
group there is the potential for great violence. Whenever a segment of the community becomes known as
the "other," the community-at-large releases its violence on that "other." Frequently, the targets of this
violence are the people who have disturbed the peace,

the norm, the system. That the status quo has been disturbed is especially evident in Africa. African women are primarily expected to bear children, to care for the home, and to farm the fields. Children are the farm laborers, but many have become ill with AIDS. They too have upset the norm. Even children are now identified as "other." Dr. Cecile de Sweemer of Senegal has said that often an entire community will drive out of their midst the children and women with AIDS, forcing them to go off to die alone and without any medical treatment.[1] *Us and them.*

The reality is, *we have AIDS.* There are still some who preach from the vantage point of the righteous "we," and look at those of us who have AIDS and say, *"They* are getting what they deserve. This is God's wrath." I have spent long hours of soul-searching and theological reflection along my journey. The images that arise in my mind are of the women and children and all the persons I have known who have AIDS. I want to rise up before those who would preach that word and say, "How dare you! How dare you call those people the 'them,' the 'other'—how dare you drive them away from the God who loves them?" As long as AIDS patients are treated as marginalized people, society's throwaways, then AIDS will continue to be a vehicle of the division of *us and them.*

AIDS is a reality. It does not discriminate. It is striking African women and children, African-Americans, I.V. drug users, hemophiliacs, and gays. The majority of these persons can be categorized as a marginal "them." But I tell you tonight that my experience with God and my understanding of the gospel is that with God there are no disposable human beings. With God there is no "other." God welcomes all. Each person is precious in God's sight. Every child of God is of infinite worth, whether that person is diseased or healthy.

We have AIDS. The world community suffers with AIDS and God's love knows no boundaries. The intention of God is that humanity might be drawn together in love so that we can say, especially as the church, *we have AIDS*, and we will journey together.

DOING THEOLOGY

When the twentieth-century church admits that we have AIDS, our way of doing theology will also change. At the Toronto Consultation on AIDS in October, 1987, jointly sponsored by the World Council of Churches and the National Council of Churches in the U.S.A. and Canada, Kevin Gordon delivered a paper in which he asked, "Is theology possible after AIDS?"[2] He reminded us that several major catastrophes in this century have radically altered our way of "doing theology": Hiroshima, Auschwitz, and the possibility of nuclear holocaust. What about AIDS? How do we do theology in the midst of AIDS? Will our traditional, neat answers to questions about suffering and the meaning of human life prove adequate?

Peter Berger identifies two methods of doing theology. One method is inductive, moving from the human experience to make statements about God. The other method is deductive, and commences with assertions and presuppositions about God and then relates the human situation to these statements.[3] With AIDS, and perhaps in any crisis, if we use only deductive faith, starting with traditional God-talk, we are at risk in our faith. Our discovery or conclusions may be of a God who is wrathful and vengeful with so-called sinners. I am convinced that theology is neither inductive nor deductive; it is both. In my journey some of the old traditional confessions of faith—simple statements about God: God is love, God loves unconditionally, with God there are no differences—have strengthened me and enabled me to move on. These confessions were embedded in me as a child in Sunday school. They undergird my experience of God now. I also find a new revelation of God in our experience of AIDS. We are beginning to understand God in new and inspired ways. The unconditional love of God can be experienced through the very ones who have formerly been named the marginal "other."

I know the eternal lover of my soul because I have known Richard, Fran, Brenda, John, Ron, Oscar, Michael, Will, Ben, and so many others. I know God because I have known these persons. *We have AIDS.* Possibly the persons with AIDS among us are the learned rabbis of this age. We have AIDS, and we are learning new lessons about both God and ourselves. We are learning something new about healing. Healing is different from a cure. At the Toronto AIDS consultation, we talked about this very thing. What is the difference between healing and a cure? A cure is a high-tech medical conquest of disease. Healing becomes possible when a person moves toward wholeness. And I must tell you that those of us with AIDS are learning about healing. We are being healed: healed of old broken relationships, healed of painful self-images, healed of our burdensome guilt. We are experiencing and learning something about healing. It is possible to be healed without being cured.

These healing moments are sacramental, an act of grace. This very moment reflects God's grace. That moment you squeeze my hand is a moment of grace; likewise the five minutes I play with my cats Earlene, Oolong, and Captain Floyd; the joy of a pizza shared with my roommates; the spontaneous hugs that I received at the opening of the Commission on Faith and Order last night. We live in a moment of grace. We are learning as people how to be joyful in the midst of a crisis. Would you have believed when you came in and started singing tonight that gathered here is a people who are going through a terrible crisis? We sing as if we've already gone to heaven.

So we are learning to live in joy. We are learning about liberation. We can't really be free until we have entered the struggle. The dawn of my liberation—my personal liberation—is finally coming. I have spent a lifetime wrestling with the angel of struggle. I have been freed and sent on with a blessing. We are also learning about peace in the midst of our fears. Our anger *can* be transformational. We discover that compassion knows no color, gender, age, or lifestyle. Our humanity makes us one. In all this, we are learning more about the resurrection.

I will never forget the first time that I experienced the quilt, "The Names Project," in Washington, D.C.; it was three football fields large and still growing. I walked onto that quilt and immediately I knew, once and for all, that the resurrection is real. I experienced the presence of thousands of people who have gone before us, and they said to me, "It will be OK." We are learning more about resurrection possibilities. We encounter modern-day saints among us: caregivers (some whom I know personally—the Davies Hospital staff; Jean, Dana, Nora, Gene, David, Jim), Lynn, my pastor Jim Mitulski, David Peck; those in the Unity and Renewal study group of the [National Council of Churches] Commission on Faith and Order. These are saints among us—and we are learning to accept their gifts. The list goes on. *We have AIDS.*

We are mothers who sit in the pews listening to the preaching of the Word, knowing that we are losing a child to AIDS. *We have AIDS.* We are life-mates faced with the reality that one day we will be alone. *We have*

AIDS. We are theologians grappling with the issue of suffering and humanity. *We have AIDS.* We have AIDS in this moment of history. God calls us as the people of God to be ministers of compassion. God calls us to be prophetic where there is injustice and suffering. God gives us the gift of ears to listen, perhaps more so in this time than ever before. We listen more than we expound. God calls the church, the church that has AIDS, to be a safe and supportive place.

At the Toronto AIDS consultation, one study stream delivered a powerful statement; truly a statement of faith. I would like to share part of that with you in closing.

"The questions surrounding AIDS are often ambiguous and the answers often inadequate. Nonetheless, each individual and each church must struggle with this uncertainty. To do nothing is to make a profound statement about the nature of illness and health in our society. Silence can be deadly. Persons with AIDS and those with HIV infection are among us and not separate from us. The crisis of AIDS is our crisis. It is not a 'we/they' issue. The church must share in this experience, changing and being changed so as to enable society to provide a supporting presence for those who are grieving and suffering."

We have AIDS. "Faced with the present urgency, we as a global community recognize our brokenness and common need for healing and reconciliation. Together as a community we must continue to struggle toward genuine acceptance of and respect for each individual person. To do this, we must overcome prejudice and discrimination. We are not called to be judgmental. We are called to be a healing church. We believe that all people are equal before God. AIDS is a disease that highlights the fragmented nature of our world. It frightens many into a response of isolation, injustice, and abandonment of those in need. Such responses are contrary to the scriptural mandate of reconciliation. AIDS challenges us into a new level of introspection and communication that releases the energy of human hope, courage and love. The supreme challenge of AIDS is for the church truly to be God's agent of love and reconciliation in the world."[4]

We, the body of Christ, in this moment of history, have AIDS. We have a loving, tender, merciful, and compassionate God who walks with us on our journey. Amen.

2 *Ron Russell-Coons*

Letters to Connie

SAN FRANCISCO, JANUARY 9, 1989—Awake at five-thirty this morning, I knew I would finally begin the process of writing. It has been almost two months since I received this assignment at a meeting of the Commission on Faith and Order of the National Council of the Churches of Christ, U.S.A. I represent persons with AIDS and my own faith communion in the Study Group on the Unity of the Church and the Renewal of the Human Community. Recently I began to sense that I might be disappointing three groups: the Unity and Renewal group, persons with AIDS, and my church. I wanted to make a responsible and articulate contribution, but since Thanksgiving Day, 1988, I have been unable to function either mentally or physically in my usual self-confident manner. I spend two to three hours daily in the Outpatient Infusion Center of R. K. Davies Hospital in San Francisco, where I receive a toxic antifungal medication. For the remaining hours of the day, I try to recuperate from sedatives administered during my infusions.

And so this project had been delayed, and once again I have experienced the frustration of living with AIDS. But even though I didn't have the energy to write, ideas were plentiful in those long hospital hours.

Now I am determined to rise to the challenge. Hopefully there will be a helpful discussion about the church's role in the AIDS crisis. We will have another glimpse of the possibility of unity in the church and the renewal of the human community. AIDS may well be the catalyst for the latter.

November, 1987

Dear Connie,

I am trying desperately to understand the emotions and feelings of our family. Sometimes I get so angry with all of you. Why can't you accept the fact that I have AIDS? That I suffer from a life-threatening virus? That I need your love and support?

Other times I possess a more analytical frame of mind. I know that my disease is embarrassing for you. "My little brother has the gay disease! My brother has a sexually transmitted disease . . . STD . . . VD!" And, while you say the words "I love you," you are mad as hell with me. AIDS deprives us of the opportunity to shield or cover up. I guess you could tell your friends I have cancer or another "acceptable" disease. But for you to admit I have AIDS would translate for most people to mean that your brother is gay, a drug user, or bisexual. In a very real sense, my illness has brought the family "out of the closet."

Say it. Tell me you are furious. I invite this because I long for you to move through your anger to a level of acceptance. Then maybe you can be the sister I need. Remember when we were kids and had to wash the dishes every night? How I wish we could stand in front of the sink right this very minute and wash a huge pile of dirty dishes. We could once again innocently and safely share our dreams and fears. We would nurture, support, and protect each other.

But I am here, twenty-five hundred miles away in Seattle, on this bleak November day. The reality hurts. We are so spiritually separated by walls and barriers.

With honesty and love,

Ron

December, 1987

Dear Connie,

Hopefully your Thanksgiving Day was filled with an abundance of food and love. I missed my family. Remember past Thanksgiving Days on Grandma's farm? How did she ever produce such culinary masterpieces with twelve grandchildren underfoot? The sights, sounds, and smells of those reunions seem more vivid for me these days. I guess it is part of the process of sorting through my life and focusing on the more life-giving and substantial moments and dimensions.

This Thanksgiving Day I got a reprieve from my daily I.V. injection of Amphotericin B. Since they increased the dosage, I have felt quite weak. The remedy, according to my friends, is to eat . . . *all the time!* My therapist invited us to a celebration where they had prepared a huge bowl of mashed potatoes in my honor, all because I mentioned my craving for them. The craving has now ceased!

Tomorrow I have outpatient surgery to have a Groshong catheter implanted in my chest. Last week a nurse was accidentally stuck while inserting an I.V. needle into my arm. We both panicked! She tried hard not to show her fear and wanted to calm me down. However, she clearly felt alarmed. Using the little information that I have, I told her to rub a mild solution of bleach on the source of the bleeding. Now it's wait and see. There is no reason for her to be tested until after ninety days. Never do I want to experience that horror again; thus the decision to have the catheter. It appears that I may be on the I.V. drug through the Christmas holidays.

You asked if I am depressed. The real answer is yes; on some days, at some moments. I go through the bargaining. I ask, "Why me?" There are times I feel isolated, even though someone is usually here. Mother sent me an old quilt that Grandma made. When I wrap up in it, I sense a great peacefulness. I imagine Grandma's strong, nurturing arms around me. Then I know that I can manage to live through this.

Happy Christmas shopping!

Ron

January, 1988

Dear Connie,

Once again the faith issue is resurrected. Hear me; please, hear me! I know that I am God's child and that divine love is at work within me. While I may be dealing with esphoglitis and zosters, I am experiencing incredible inner healing. It may sound absurd, but AIDS has been the catalyst for healing.

My "coming out" meant that many people got hurt. I divorced my wife of nine years and left two beautiful children. You too were affected, and our parents were emotionally crushed. I carried a tremendous burden of guilt. My guilt often broadened to areas and things over which I had no control or responsibility. But I felt the guilt! Finally, in these last few months, I have been able to forgive myself and my past. What a gift of grace! This inner peace is from God.

So your prayers and concerns can change. Instead of asking God to change my sexual orientation and then, incidentally, to heal my illness, you can thank God for the healings I am experiencing deep within. My faith is full and strong. The negatives of the virus at work in my body can never overshadow the loving touch of God that heals my spirit.

Your brother in the faith,

Ron

February, 1988

My dear sister,

Happy Valentine's Day!

I returned home safely after my visit with all of you there in Alabama. Thank you for coming over to mother's house to be with me. When I left here, I didn't know if you would visit. It must be very difficult to overcome all of your fears concerning AIDS. The media certainly doesn't help the situation; many times they sensationalize AIDS rather than offer correct information. Anyway, I sensed that you were more comfortable, and I felt like we had quality time together.

Seeing my children was both wonderful and frightening. They have grown into remarkable individuals. I am quite proud of them. However, I couldn't help wondering if I will ever see them again. As they drove away, I stood on the porch and tried to envision our next meeting. The sadness eased as I focused on another, future visit. How will they look? Will they like me any better?

My immediate future involves yet another trip to the hospital. As you saw, the zoster on my forehead is worsening. I will be receiving I.V. Acyclovir and morphine for the pain. Please, God, help me with this intense pain. Since I don't want to scratch the blisters open, I wear gloves or a white sock over my hands. I have to scratch. I have to endure.

Say a prayer for me!

With love,

Ron

June, 1988

Dear Connie,

I should be accustomed to change by now. However, I continue to fight and resist changes. During the last year, each change has meant letting go of something so vitally important to me. One major change has occurred.

In mid-May, I realized I could no longer function under the normal everyday stresses of professional ministry. I delegated responsibilities to an assistant pastor. Then the church opted for a copastorate. But I was unable to carry my share of duties. Finally, after sorting through my own feelings about letting go of my pastoral role, I discussed the matter with my physician and close friend, Jim. He expressed genuine surprise that I had not sought a disability leave six months earlier. He revealed that my determination had been an inspiration to him. We never can predict how our lives impact on others. I had always concentrated on the negative ways I might affect people. How refreshing to learn that my life brought joy and inspiration to another!

I became a "retired pastor" on June 5. The church held a special service in my honor. My therapist, therapy group, doctor, nurses, and a host of friends came to wish me well and express their support. It was a moment of thanksgiving, grace, and renewal. I said that I was ready to "let go." But it has been hard. Though I can rationalize by saying that I'll now have a new type of specialized AIDS ministry, I know I'll never again be a pastor of a church. This is difficult and painful for me to accept. I need strength.

Please let me know that you are with me in thought and that you care. I appreciate your letters.

Your loving brother,

Ron

July, 1988

Dear Connie,

What a month! I celebrated my fortieth birthday just as I ended my first full month of retirement (disability leave). So many projects await me. I want to write and to share my journey as a person living with AIDS. My journal is full of the expected ups and downs, with numerous notations describing how my faith and ministry have sustained me. So why do I feel empty today?

Chuck wrestles with his plans for a profession and how that fits into our life together. It's got to be hard living with someone who has AIDS. Yes, even I can be a cranky patient. I know that there are times when I am subconsciously beginning to pull away; this is undoubtedly a kind of preparation for death.

Last week is a blur. I was hospitalized once again for the zoster and this time Demerol was prescribed for the pain. At first my amnesia was so profound that I couldn't remember who visited me. Slowly I am putting it back together. The memory lapses frighten me.

Once, when coming home on the bus, I suddenly forgot where I was going and where we lived. I wandered around on streets that I had walked down dozens of times. Nothing looked familiar. How I kept calm through that I'll never know. When I look back on it, I shudder with fear. Please, God, don't let me lose my mind. Fear of dementia is strong for me. I've seen too many parishioners with AIDS get to the point where they are curled up in a fetal position, totally unaware of their environment.

I miss the church. Surely most persons with AIDS have moments when they yearn to resume their careers. For me, being a pastor was more than just a job. It was my community, my intentional family here in Seattle.

In order to facilitate the "letting go" on my part and theirs, I have tried to limit my contacts with people from the church. I'm lonely and sad today. I will go forward and find that place of peace. God is with me and you!

Ron

September, 1988

Dear Connie,

Gail, my therapist, wrote an affirmation that I now try to live by daily: "You can do whatever you need to live the rest of your life fully." Remaining in Seattle was too painful. Constant reminders that my pastoral ministry had ended surrounded me. Chuck had received an invitation to work as an intern with the Names Project in San Francisco. And so we packed our belongings and loaded our three cats, Floyd, Earlene, and Oolong, and headed for the city by the bay. We are doing what we need "to live the rest of our lives fully."

I almost expected to find a city enshrouded with despair and depression. Instead, San Francisco seems to have caught on to what it means to be in this crisis together. There is a true sense of "we-ness" about San Francisco's AIDS epidemic. I'm happy to be here. Most churches in the bay area have moved beyond exercising moral judgment in this crisis and are engaged in AIDS ministry. The Metropolitan Community Church on Eureka Street has a monthly AIDS healing service. During the holidays, a group from the Golden Gate Church of the Nazarene began attending those services. I never thought that I would see the day when Nazarenes would worship, even receive Communion, together with gays and lesbians from the Metropolitan Community Church. Indeed, I thought the Parousia had occurred. Perhaps the universal church could learn from that wonderful ecumenical moment. We were focused on prayers of healing rather than on our theological differences. The hymn "It Is

Well with My Soul" has never sounded so wonderful as it
did that night!

Please visit us anytime. You are precious to me!

With love,

Ron

3 *John*

A Journey
Toward Freedom

When the call came from Archie's parents, I signaled
to the others. We stepped into the corridor and tried
not to listen while he told them he had just been diagnosed with *pneumocystis carinii* pneumonia, one of the
opportunistic infections common in those suffering
from Acquired Immune Deficiency Syndrome. What
we had feared for months, what we had been afraid to
say even to ourselves over the past two years of his
failing health, was now upon us. Archie had AIDS.

When we came back into the room, Archie's damna-
ble composure had finally collapsed. Even his cold and
decorous sense of his own drama had failed him. He
was drawn and pale, sobbing helplessly and fighting for
breath, lying there at the center of a tangle of tubes
and hoses that snaked away from his arms and face out
to bottles and oxygen tanks standing on either side of
the bed. We had no words for him then and I can think
of no appropriate ones now. There was only the help-
less silence and the sound of air convulsively sucked
through the mask as he fought for breath enough to
weep. We couldn't have spoken in any case, standing
there around the bed, our own brave faces trembling
and wet, each of us weeping quietly, awkwardly, apart.
Then, not knowing what else to do, having stopped

thinking of what to do, one of us reached over and put her hands on his side. And without thought we all did the same, laying hands on his head, his hands, his feet; the five or six of us one by one touching the suffering body of our dear friend, holding him together until he quieted.

When he could finally speak, he spoke bitterly of his rage at the injustice of having to tell one's parents one is dying. "No parent should have to hear that from their child," he said, his voice strong and clear and loud. "It isn't right." He stopped for a moment, breathing rapidly. I remember thinking I had never seen anyone so human as he was then, so naked, so without recourse to any of the fictions that had sustained him for so long. When he spoke again, even the anger had forsaken him. What was left was a pure and deep sadness, the kind that comes when one speaks for the first time thoughts that one has hidden even from oneself and that are revealed only as they are spoken. "Isn't it sad," he said softly. "It was easier to tell them that I'm dying than it was to tell them that I'm gay."

I don't remember much after that. I know we said what we could, which wasn't much, and that we left, our arms around each other as we walked to the elevator and out into the night. In the cab, alone with a stranger, driving through the rain, I realized how right Archie had been. He had articulated something that had been, until the moment he said it, the idea that ruled him. He had believed, during all of his thirty-odd years of believing, that his parents would rather he were dead than gay. And I knew that, in the manner of children, he had taken that perception of his parents' belief and made it his own. With some mixture of sadness and hope, I realized as the cab drove through the rain that until that night Archie would rather have been dead than be who he was.

Much has changed since those early days of the struggle. Treatments and prospects have improved; many now believe that HIV infection may not be the death sentence we once thought it was. But Archie was the first person close to me to be diagnosed. While he was not the last and even though a lot has changed, in many ways I think of his diagnosis as prefiguring what would happen among us. His story, at least as I read it now, is at once the story of his oppression and the story of his liberation, in the sense that the oppression of AIDS revealed to Archie the oppression he had experienced his whole life, and in that revelation were the beginnings of his liberation. In what follows, I will describe what I see as the three stages in Archie's liberation, stages that I believe roughly parallel the stages faced by the gay community. Then I will turn to how the church might best be with us as we come into our freedom.

PERSONAL FREEDOM

The first stage of gay liberation occurs at the personal, psychological level, precisely because that is where we have so keenly felt our oppression. Integration—which is at this stage another word for liberation—begins to happen when we articulate our gay identity to ourselves, and it continues as we begin to articulate it to others. Often the others are our parents, but not always. Whomever we speak to, our liberation depends on understanding how our oppression has operated in the past, in our relationships with our peers, our siblings, and especially our parents.

The experience of being loved by one's parents is so primary, so essential, so longed for and yet so rare, that we often try to bypass it, telling ourselves that concerns for parental approval are unbecoming for mature adults. Such is the nature of our particular oppression, however, that gay men and lesbians are not allowed an adolescence wherein parental approval begins to be replaced with the love and acceptance of our partners, of society, and of ourselves for ourselves. For us, our parents often remain the first citizens of a world that hates us, and so their response to us, stated or unstated, becomes emblematic of the world's response. Therefore, our attempts to fight our way back into the world often focus what seems to be a disproportionate amount of attention on our relationship with our parents. Our liberation need not mean "winning" their approval, nor does it necessarily mean coming out to them, but it must include making our peace with them, however uneasy such a peace may be. And there can be no ignorant peace; the first feature of Archie's epiphany was the realization of how painful his history with his parents had been. His peace was found only on the far side of honest struggle. Liberation may be as simple as forgiving the past, but if it is a forgiveness that does not name what has happened then it is not forgiveness at all and there can be no liberation in it.

In Archie's case, after the epiphany described above, the man who had so harshly judged himself was reborn as a warm, open, creative human being. For the first time, he allowed himself to be loved—by his partner, his friends, his parents, and himself, and by God. He began to rid himself of the notion that his parents would rather he was dead than gay, and in so doing he began to throw off his own childhood appropriation of that unstated dread. His parents, after all, by continuing to love him, proved to him that this was not the case.

I believe that the self-worth Archie found gave rise to a sense of justice that is the hallmark of liberation at this stage. Before we begin to value ourselves, the abuse we experience seems intolerable, but it also seems strangely expected; if we hate ourselves enough, the abuse may seem deserved, even desired. After Archie began to accept the love around him, he could no longer accept that abuse. That refusal to be abused not only freed him to act but also protected him from hateful reactions to his actions. When he began to tell his story publicly, he received quite a lot of hate mail. He was able to retain his sense of freedom and purpose because he now knew, in his heart of hearts, that the letter writers were wrong. His belief in his own worth had become belief in the justice of his cause. He told me once that he had even discovered some compassion for those who reviled him, because he had come to believe that their hate wounded them far more than it did him.

Archie's personal freedom to live and to love happened because, in a moment of intense anguish, he was granted the grace to know that he was loved. He was lucky. He had friends and family around to show him love. Many are not so fortunate, and for them it is even more difficult. But, grace being what it is, sometimes the knowledge of love can happen even when human love abandons us entirely. I don't understand it, but I believe it can happen. And, however it happens, knowing we are loved grounds us in a standard of value that cannot be limited to the private and the personal. The new worth we feel for ourselves grows into a sense of what is valuable in all human life. When that connection between the private and the social spheres is made, then lasting liberation can be ours, because real freedom is not just freedom for ourselves, but freedom to live our lives for others. When we begin to make the connection between love and justice in our own lives and love and justice for all people, then we are free to move to the next stage in our liberation. We are free to act.

ACTION

The second stage of gay liberation is the action that follows, or accompanies, the internal struggle. On one level, this may simply mean authentic sexual behavior in a mutual, loving, committed relationship. The importance of such private action cannot be minimized; it is, however, when this private action is made public that its political import becomes more apparent. For gay men and lesbians in this society, to bring one's life partner to the Christmas dance at the office constitutes a political act, as does a refusal to come unless he or she is invited. Indeed, any demonstration of one's private affectional commitments has political force in a society that persists in denying the legitimacy of our relationships. Of course it is tiresome to have one's relationships so consistently politicized, but I have found no healthy alternative. The cost of remaining private with our relationships is too great and is itself a political choice. The private heart cannot be separated from the public self. As humans, we are social creatures, and to ask gay men and lesbians to be anything less than fully social is to ask us to be less than fully human.

The second level of action is more explicitly and traditionally political. We were just beginning to learn something of this before we were faced with the AIDS crisis. In 1969, at a bar called Stonewall in New York City, gay men responded to police harassment with a full-scale riot. In that grand and violent cracking of the closet door, we learned something of what we had to do for ourselves. We had to break through the personal and cultural denial that kept us trapped in ghettos and double lives. Some political activism began in those years; certainly gay culture became much more visible and vocal between 1969 and 1982. But in many ways our struggle remained a private affair, shared perhaps with a few others most like us, but rarely daring to come together with those who were different. We didn't do much in those years to combat homophobia in the culture; most of the time, we were fighting only for our right to be left alone. Nor were we entirely comfortable even with each other. Race and class divided us. Even the visible markers of our own identity divided us; those who could pass as straight wouldn't be caught dead with those who could not. But AIDS began to change that; in a sense, AIDS caught us dead and showed us how to live.

What happened to the gay community in the context of the AIDS struggle will be a subject for analysis long after the virus has been conquered. Untying that knot is certainly beyond the scope of this discussion. But however complex the causes that came together in those early days of the struggle, the net effect was that AIDS revealed to us how very much we wanted to be alive. We had been caught dead; from now on, we vowed, we would only be *found living.* In Archie's case, the sense of justice that had grown out of his new feeling of self-worth led him into the public arena. During the two and a half years following his diagnosis, he became a well-known spokesperson, an articulate advocate, and a committed educator. He even became something of a national figure, when National Public Radio began following his case in regular features. Of course it wasn't easy. The response was sometimes hateful, but it was also, sometimes, loving; people were touched by his struggle, and even identified with his pain.

Like Archie, our community has learned to act for justice. However imperfect the advancement of our struggle—and it will always be imperfect—we have begun the process of translating our freedom into action. In doing so we have learned to come together. We had to come together in order to care for our sick, to fight for our cures, to bury our dead. None among us doubted that if we did not take care of each other then no one else would—not families, not friends, not the church, not the medical establishment, and certainly not the government. The alienation we had experienced since our youth, that private separation that we had just begun to share with even a few close friends, was now a public and political cause. As a community, we were learning to live with AIDS. We, who hadn't even been able to say "we" before, are living with AIDS.

DEATH

This is the hard part. Archie died in August of last year. The news reached me at my parents' home in Arkansas. When I explained what had happened to Archie, my parents asked the obvious question about my own health. I had not planned to tell them, and I certainly never expected them to ask, but in that moment it did not occur to me to lie. And so I told them about my own HIV-positive status, about my fears, and about my faith. My mother wept. My father sat silently in the corner while Mom left the room. "You know," he said, "this is hard for us to understand." I said, "Yes, I know." And we sat there, in silence, until my mother returned. Which doesn't sound much like a liberation, but, strangely, it was, if only because it was honest.

I had spent a great deal of time with Archie in his last days, watching him fight to his last hope, and watching him fade once the last hope was gone. He went gracefully, as he lived. With the help of his lover Drew, he decided to remove the feeding tube, to leave the apartment and go to the museum and then to a

movie, and then he left his body while in his lover's
arms, as we all should. I know that he thought he was
going somewhere, or at least that he hoped so. He had,
however, reached a point where it no longer mattered
so much; even if there were no heaven, it was better
than this hell. And so he went wherever he went, and
wherever he went I hope he's free.

As I have suggested, the imminence of our mortality
has taught us a great deal about living, and that has
been liberating. In this sense, death is liberating because of its finality; because it is the hard, unmovable
boundary of our lives that frames all our days. Because
we know now that no trick of the mind will relieve us
of our mortality, we have learned to live fully in the
time we have. Of course, that means living with our
pain as much as it means living with our joy. We know
better than most how the two can be commingled. For
us, the joyful ache of laughter, shared with friends who
will be gone too soon, is never far removed from the
great grief we feel when they do go. But we live it all,
the joy and the pain, as best we can—fully, even voraciously, knowing that every moment, joyful or painful,
is a gift. On our worst days, we live in fear. On our
best, we live without it, because we have named it and
seen it and borne it together. We remember when we
bore it alone, when there wasn't a "we" and when we
couldn't even say what "it" was. What we bear now is
painful beyond expression, just as it is joyful beyond
words, because now it is the living pain of a community
learning to love itself, not the dead pain of cultural and
personal denial, and it is in the painful life of our community that we now claim the joy of our salvation.

But as we live with AIDS and as we claim salvation in
our struggle, there are those among us who die of AIDS.
They are not victims; we do our best to be sure that
they live with AIDS before they die from it. But they do

die. And they keep dying. If the knowledge of death can be described as liberating, can the *fact* of death be liberating, too? For Archie, I believe it was. But for most of us, I'm not so sure. Having discarded traditional notions of life after death, some have turned to New Age thought and its appropriation of Eastern beliefs in reincarnation. Most of us lack any vision of what will happen to us after we die. The mainline church has been no help at all; it has been no more able to talk about death than it has been able to talk about sexuality. The enormity of that failure is staggering.

CHALLENGING THE CHURCH

As we integrate our lives, as we bring those lives into committed action and as we face our death, we need the church. Because being loved is how most of us learn to feel worth loving, we need the church to love us. To love us *in spite of* our sexuality is not enough; the church must love us, as God does, *because* we are gay. Until the church can affirm that our sexuality is part of God's perfect will for our lives, it will continue to participate in a culture that keeps us in unfreedom. Nor is a simple change of attitude enough. As it was with Archie and his family, there can be no real healing without confronting the past. Reconciliation can happen only when the church faces for itself the damage it has done.

When our lives become integrated enough to become public, the church must be there to help us proclaim the victory. Particularly when we commit our relationships before God, the church can join with us and with the whole community of faith in celebrating the joy of our shared lives. Of course that means blessing our unions, but it also means the kind of support and nurture offered other families. Even when we do not join together as a couple in the traditional sense, the church can help us as we recognize the sanctity of all our relationships.

If the church can join us as we actively live free and integrated lives, it can then join us in our communal struggle. Once we become ill, many of us have no homes, or we have no care in our homes if we live alone. Transportation, clothing, medication, conversation, fun—the list of these needs is almost endless. As an advocate, the church could be invaluable, particularly because it has been the traditional ally of our enemies. Nor would this new alliance be a one-way street. I suspect that the church would benefit from it more than we would.

As we learn to live together, perhaps then we can begin to learn together about what it means to die, because that's where we need the most help. In our community, the newfound sense of life's fullness has brought us to the point where we believe again in the meaning of our lives. But as rich as our lives have become, the magnitude of our struggle takes its toll, and it often seems that death will overwhelm the new life among us. Belief in meaning is not enough to sustain us in the struggle. That meaning needs substance, form, narrative. We tell our own stories, but that isn't enough. We need something we can turn to other than our own experience to give us strength.

As a Christian, I believe that the story of Jesus could offer narrative substance to the meaning we have already discovered—because Jesus is crucified as we are, because Jesus dies as we do, and because Jesus rises again into newness of life, *as we will.* The liberation of that promise can scarcely be exaggerated in a community where death is so near and so real.

Unfortunately, the history of the gay community with the church makes it nearly impossible for us to claim the promise. The church has rightly recognized through the ages that the promise reveals itself in the life of the community of faith. To be cut off from that community is, in a sense, to be cut off from the promise. Of course, we reject this. We are not cut off. We have our own community, we have learned our own faith and we have even formed our own churches. Still, how difficult it is for us to hold onto the promise of God when the institution that claims to be the body of Christ denies us a place in its community.

We are challenging the church to celebrate life and all that expresses life, especially sexuality. And we are challenging the church to talk about death, including the promise of life after death. The old metaphors of pearly gates and golden streets have flattened into a joke. Nor will promises that we will be free of the flesh help us much; they only deny our life and love here. What about the resurrection of the body? What about eternal life? We know something of what these mean in our life *before* death—in fact, we may be able to help the church understand more about that—but what does it mean about life *after* death? We need to hear these promises interpreted for us. We need to know that we will not be forgotten, that God will gather us into God's bosom, that this day we shall be with God in paradise.

Archie was a remarkable person. Through the support of his community and family, he managed to believe that freedom awaited him when he died. Archie found his "church" outside the church. How tragic that the community of baptized believers could have no part in Archie's liberation, either in his life or in his death. How immeasurably impoverished the church will be if it can not include all who struggle along the road of life. I have been speaking from the gay male perspective. Many others struggle with AIDS, and they too have been excluded by the church. Our liberation is all bound up together; not one of us will be free until we all are free. For all of us, salvation will mean, as it always has, coming into the embrace of God. That happens right here, right now, in this life after birth as we are all taken up into the arms of God's church. And later, when the inevitable comes, through AIDS or old age or however it happens, we need to claim the promise of God that life is eternal.

In this age of AIDS, we are doing nothing more or less than challenging the church to be the church. When it can proclaim the glad tidings of great joy *which shall be to all people,* then it will be the church it is called to be. To do anything less is to betray the one who suffered, died, and rose again that *all* might have life, and have it more abundantly.

A Church Renewed

The spiral of theological engagement continues in Part Two, as members of the Unity and Renewal study group respond to the experiences of living with AIDS, such as those in Part One. The responses in no way exhaust the subject. Like the life stories in chapters 1 through 3 and 10, they represent the research of one ecumenical group that focused its energy on the gay community. We did so because we had the opportunity and privilege, and because there was so much to learn in just this one area. We in no way intended to ignore the pressing needs and experiences of struggle to be found among I.V. drug users, women, children, hemophiliacs, and other persons infected by the virus.

The study group met together and reflected on the areas where we were learning clues to church renewal from life experiences with AIDS. There were four areas where possibilities for renewal could be discerned. The first three areas are described in Part Two, and include a new understanding of hospitality, of non-dualistic interpretation of scriptural and church tradition, and of the nature of sin as oppression. The fourth area was the importance of justice as a perspective for understanding the nature of the church. This is explored in Part Three.

67

In chapter 4, "Space for Hospitality and Hope," Beryl Ingram-Ward shares the experience of her visit to the Metropolitan Community Church of San Francisco, where she attended an ecumenical AIDS healing service with other members of the study group and the Commission on Faith and Order. This overwhelming experience of hospitality from the very persons who had been rejected by most of the churches represented at the service leads her to reflect on what it means, in Hebrews 13:13, when believers are exhorted to go forth "outside the camp" to join Christ among those who are suffering and rejected.

Chapter 5 deals with the issues of dualistic interpretations of body and spirit; church and world. Arthur Freeman discusses issues in biblical interpretation in the light of the dualism contained in many parts of the biblical message. He urges reinterpretation of dualistic biblical and church traditions in the light of the way those traditions have allowed the church to ignore the social and physical needs of persons in the name of a "higher" spiritual good. The implications of this separation become apparent in chapter 6, "Oppression and Resurrection Faith," where Susan E. Davies shows how separation of personal sins from sinful structures of society allows the church to ignore justice issues. Learning how to face the fears of sexuality, death, and difference can be a clue to the renewal of the church, but to move in this direction, our resurrection faith must be rooted in an incarnational commitment to share in the suffering of those living with AIDS.

4   *Beryl Ingram-Ward*

Space
for Hospitality and Hope

It was an amazing worship service. What occurred
that night was such a surprise and revelation for me
that I have chosen to write about it not as a critical
analysis but as a simple reflection through the lens of
Hebrews 13:12–13: "So Jesus also suffered outside the
gate in order to sanctify the people through his own
blood. Therefore let us go forth to him outside the
camp, and bear the abuse he endured."

Most of my life is lived "inside the gate," sheltered
and secure. I function on a day-to-day basis with no
conscious awareness of being an "insider" unless I
move through that invisible wall that divides the "insiders" from the "outsiders" and discover that I am
outside.

Several times I have practiced what Henri Nouwen
calls "voluntary displacement." In 1968, I went to Ni-
geria, and in 1986 to Nicaragua with Witness for
Peace. Particularly in Nicaragua, I was "outside the
camp," visiting war-torn villages in the countryside.
Whenever I venture outside the camp, the world of
insiders and outsiders is turned inside out, and epiphany (that is, God revealed) is the order of the day.

In March, 1989, I was part of a group of pilgrims
moving outside the gate for just a few hours; hours that

69

opened my eyes to a new way of seeing this wounded world God is redeeming.

The Unity and Renewal study group of the Commission on Faith and Order (COFO) of the National Council of Churches has been wrestling with the AIDS issue and its impact on the unity and renewal of the church. Usually we work with case studies. In this case, we became part of one. Because our March meeting was scheduled for Burlingame, California, a city near San Francisco, the Rev. Ron Russell-Coons was asked to coordinate a worship experience where the entire commission could worship with persons with AIDS (PWAs). Russell-Coons is on the pastoral staff of Metropolitan Community Church of San Francisco and, with Pastor Jim Mitulski's blessing, invited all of us to attend the weekly Friday night healing service at his church. The church is in San Francisco's Castro District, home to one of the largest gay populations in the world.

In the world of insiders and outsiders, straights are "inside" and gays are "outside." Persons without AIDS are "inside," and PWAs are "outside." Many denominations with recognizable names are "inside," and the Universal Fellowship of Metropolitan Community Churches is "outside."

The denomination was started in 1968 by a gay former Pentecostal minister, the Rev. Troy Perry. He established a church whose purpose was to gather in the outsiders and to create a safe and hospitable place for them, a church whose doors would be open to all of God's children without distinction or discrimination. Approximately 80 percent of the membership of UFMCC is lesbian or gay.

In 1981 the church applied for membership in the National Council of Churches (NCC). After all, it was doing significant ministry in the name of Jesus. The UFMCC met all the requirements for membership in the NCC: it had a trinitarian faith; it was organized on a national level with more than the necessary number of members and local congregations; and it had a viable program of mission and a theological training program. Still, its application for membership was tabled, because its position on human sexuality was judged to be unacceptable by other member denominations. Undaunted by this rejection, the UFMCC accepted the invitation to participate in several of the National Council's units, including the Commission on Faith and Order. Their ministry "outside the camp" continued to those who had been rejected by the homophobic Christian churches in which they had grown up, and not only continued, but grew. It grew because there was a need for it.

And then came AIDS. As AIDS began its relentless scourge of the gay male population, more people sought a refuge from the battering storm of misinformation, isolation, cruelty, and death. Pastor Jim Mitulski said that, in 1988, despite the high number of deaths in the MCC San Francisco congregation and the gay men's community, membership in the church grew by a third, as people seeking intimacy and spirituality found their way to this embracing congregation [ch. 11, p. 165].

It is easy to assume that this oppressed and reviled group coalesced and developed around a core of bitterness and cynicism, hostile and suspicious of outsiders from the NCC. Not so, as I discovered for myself on that amazing March evening in the heart of Lent.

What an odd sight we must have been, climbing out of the chartered bus, some seventy of us; an eclectic entourage of theologians, priests, and pastors, some collared, signatory rings and pectoral crosses announcing our presence; apprehensive comments signaling dis-ease; nervous glances and "It will be OK" smiles

buoying up ones who were saying, in body language,
"What have we gotten ourselves into?" It didn't take
long to find out.

Lyle Schaller, they read your books! Outside the
open door of the unimposing facade of the church
stood the first of the greeters welcoming us and direct-
ing us inside to the guest register and to ushers with
warm smiles, who, with sincere handshakes, said, "Hi,
I'm John (or Henry, or Gary). There's still room back
there. Front pews fill up fast here." The sanctuary was
crowded with men. It didn't take long to understand
why.

Settling into an uncomfortable wooden chair, I was
instantly captured by the music for gathering. Fifty of
the church women were gone for a weekend retreat,
so it was deeply resonant male voices blending in a
piety sweet and honest. Singing was no drudgery here;
a buoyant atmosphere filled this holy space.

The first song was "When the Roll Is Called Up Yonder, I'll Be There." I've sung that old gospel hymn
many times, and I confess I love it, but I'd never heard
it sung "outside the camp" before. I was hearing it
sung by women and men who have been told by their
original denominational homes that because of their
sexual orientation they most assuredly would *not* have
a place "up yonder" when the roll was called! Surely
they are people of sorrow and acquainted with grief.
Until the UFMCC was founded, these people had been
abused and denied a place in the body of Christ because of their sexual orientation. Here they were, in
church, singing wholeheartedly of their faith in the
faithfulness of Jesus, who was present in their midst
outside the camp. It was, for me, a thundering affirmation of God.

As I reveled in the sight and sounds of people really
worshiping, not just going through the motions, I was

caught off guard by my emotional response. Tears welled up: tears for these women and men; tears for their years of pain and shame and fear; tears for the PWAs living with certain death in their bodies; tears for their finding this haven of hope and hospitality; and tears for my own ignorance and for the narrowness of the church catholic, which continues to persecute these children of God, these sisters and brothers of Jesus who have drawn together with him outside the camp.

Among those worshiping that Passiontide night were PWAs who had come with their nurses from their hospital beds to be present. Yes, from their hospital beds! They joined as they were able in the singing:

> What have I to dread, what have I to fear,
> Leaning on the everlasting arms?
> I have blessed peace with my Lord so near,
> Leaning on the everlasting arms.
> Leaning, leaning, safe and secure from all
>   alarms;
> Leaning, leaning, leaning on the everlasting
>   arms.[1]

What have these PWAs to dread? Yes, they do face almost certain death, but some of them told us that they have passed through the worst already. The years of closeted paranoia are past. Here at MCC-SF they have found assurance that who they are is who God made them, and God made them good. Here they have found a spiritual home full of love and affirmation, laden with hugs and embraces brimming with comfort. This church is a place of acceptance and peace, and it is not just any place, it is a *church*, Christ's church, and just its existence says to the outcast and the despised, you are accepted. Paul Tillich's words were never more relevant than when applied to their ministry.

You are accepted, accepted by that which is greater

than you and the name of which you do not know. Do
not ask for the name now; perhaps you will find it later.
Do not try to do anything now; perhaps later you will
do much. Do not seek for anything; do not perform
anything; do not intend anything. Simply accept the
fact that you are accepted! If that happens to us, we
experience grace. After such an experience we may not
be better than before, and we may not believe more
than before. But everything is transformed. In that moment, grace conquers sin, and reconciliation bridges
the gulf of estrangement.[2]

"Grace conquers sin and reconciliation bridges the
gulf of estrangement": That is what I experienced in
worshiping "outside the camp" with gays, lesbians,
and persons with AIDS. MCC-SF is such a vital, loving,
accepting congregation. It is like God's easy chair,
where the leper is held with love and no one is unclean. There is a pervasive grace here communicated
through song and the church's leadership style. This
church takes God seriously. It takes scripture seriously. It takes ministry seriously. The AIDS crisis has
carved the shape of ministry for this San Francisco
congregation. As I scanned the bulletin, I was struck
by the AIDS-related ministries: four grief counseling
groups; prayer vigils; healing services; bereavement
support groups; care for the ill; home and hospital visitation; funerals and memorial services. The ministries
compose fully half of the church's programs. Members
don't have to sit around dreaming up programs for
other folks to do; the need is unmistakable, and this
congregation has said yes: yes to the homeless, yes to
the hopeless [ch. 11, p. 163]. As the hymn says, surely
the presence of the Lord is in this place.[3]

I was aware of a *kairos* moment as the community
caressed these words. Something deep inside, long
held, broke. My eyes were opened to see people in a

new way; diseased and wasting away, yes, but in this community of grace outside the camp, transformed into beauty.

The pilgrimage theology of the book of Hebrews is appropriate in this story. When the seventy of us from the COFO piled off the bus on Eureka Street, we were stepping out from the safe and known into the "unclean" and unknown. We were moving from comfort to discomfort. We were representatives of the "established" churches, and of the body that said no to this community when it asked for admission to the NCC in 1981. Some members of the COFO later confessed their confusion stemming from the healing service. I understood, because to some extent the confusion was also mine. We were insiders who had internalized prejudices of which we ourselves were unaware, until we were caught red-handed acting out of them. In moving outside the camp we went as representatives of "the one, holy, catholic and apostolic church" to a quasi-church in the diaspora. In the perceptions of some COFO members, we were the "real" church. The UFMCC didn't qualify as a "real" church. Imagine, then, our shock at discovering Christ present with the "outcasts," before we arrived! As promised in scripture, Christ was present in the midst of the worshiping community. The wholeness and the holiness overwhelmed many of us. Some of us were stunned. Long-held prejudices were exposed. Deep-rooted fears and phobias sprang to the surface and had to be confessed and dealt with.

Perhaps this is the kind of thing that happened to Nicodemus, who eventually had to sneak away from the rest of the Pharisees and come to Jesus under the cover of darkness. Nicodemus was a proper religious leader of the established religion of his day. In Jesus, the radical, he glimpsed a salvation he had not even suspected. I have a hunch that for some members of the COFO, this healing service outside the camp provided a glimpse of salvation and grace they either had never known or had forgotten in the frothy pace of classes, publications, and meetings through the years.

We went forth outside the camp, to Jesus, and his presence surprised us.

> "Be not afraid, I go before you always.
> Come, follow me and I will give you rest."[4]

With this St. Louis Jesuit song undergirding his message, the Rev. Ron Russell-Coons, our local host, preached powerfully on this passage from 2 Corinthians 4:16-18 (for sermon text, refer to chapter 1):

So we do not lose heart. Though our outer nature is wasting away, our inner nature is being renewed every day. For this slight momentary affliction is preparing for us an eternal weight of glory beyond all comparison, because we look not to the things that are seen but to the things that are unseen; for the things that are seen are transient, but the things that are unseen are eternal.

Russell-Coons ritualized the words, "We are the church, and the church has AIDS." Of course, I thought, trying to reconcile myself to this foreign concept; if one part of the body of Christ has AIDS, the body has AIDS. "For just as the body is one and has many members, and all the members of the body, though many, are one body, so it is with Christ" (1 Cor. 12:12). If one part of the body has AIDS, we are all infected, for, as Paul continues, "If one member suffers, all suffer together" (1 Cor. 12:26a). We are the church, and the church has AIDS. Along with the insightful recognition of the body of Christ with AIDS, Russell-Coons affirmed the promises of Jesus Christ, that PWAs do not walk this road alone. God is with them always. Nothing in all creation, not even AIDS, the preacher affirmed, can separate PWAs from the love of God in Christ Jesus our Lord! "Yes," I quickened. I trust those words even more now, for they came with authenticity and with power from this courageous man who is himself a PWA.

The Spirit of God was working. During the community prayers, there were requests for prayers "for my little niece, that she may someday understand"; "for my partner of eleven years, who had to return to the hospital last night"; "for my family, who are so frightened they can't even come to visit me."

Following the time of community prayer, there was a time of prayer with laying on of hands for healing. It is the custom that during this time some members of the congregation gather in teams of two across the front of the chancel, and persons seeking healing move forward to be embraced and healed by one of these pairs. It was a very publicly private space. It was a holy time. I went forward. It was uncharacteristic of me, yet in this setting of such gracious hospitality, it felt right. Here, I could name my unattended wounds, my blindness, and my homophobia, and hear compassionate voices whisper prayers for my healing. I went forward because I needed to, for not for that reason alone. I wanted to make a statement with my body, to say that I had come not just to observe others at worship, but to worship, and I was worshiping, fully present and responding to the witness of God's Spirit with my spirit.

The welcome table was spread and laden while the service proceeded [ch. 9, p. 140]. There were mounds of food to feed the congregation at the close of the service. It wasn't Eucharist, but we did feast together. As Pastor Jim Mitulski said to the worshiping community on the Sunday following this healing service, the reason there was no Eucharist was not because the commissioners were afraid to commune with UFMCC

members but because "they can't agree on it among
themselves." Funny, ironic, and true. But Eucharist or
not, in those healing moments many of us experienced
oneness around their welcome table [ch. 11, p. 172].

I knew myself a stranger welcomed into a safe space;
into a place created in God's name for hospitality and
hope. I came as a guest, and was embraced as a sister
by members of a resurrection community, for, surely,
that is what MCC-SF is; a community of the resurrection living in the very epicenter of AIDS-related death.
Every week there are two to three funerals or memorial services held at the church. It is an eschatological
community. The members are living as though the
reign of God has come; as though heaven has broken
into earth and wrested from the very jaws of death,
life; precious and profoundly God's. It is a community
of joy in the midst of tears. It is a community that can
sing songs about heaven with integrity, because it is
singing from the cross. Outside the camp, where Jesus
once suffered alone, there is a community of faith and
love, sprung up in ministry to the bruised and battered
for whom and with whom he died.

The insiders went outside, there discovered Jesus,
and the world turned inside out. "Therefore let us go
forth to him outside the camp, and bear the abuse he
endured" (Heb. 13:13).

5   *Arthur J. Freeman*

Dualism
in Christian Tradition

The spread of AIDS within our time is a crisis that may be changing our habitual way of looking at things. This crisis is an event of such magnitude that it is causing a paradigm shift, or a change in perspective. We see life through mental structures born of our experience and culture. When there are no challenges to these structures, the style of our vision persists. To change our paradigm, or way of seeing, involves not only challenges to cultural assumptions but also challenges to our internal structures, with all the threat, uncertainty, and necessity for individuation this entails. Such changes deeply touch our emotional lives, often producing great pain. We can see the history and the difficulty of paradigm changes in both science and religion in Hans Küng's *Theology for the Third Millennium.*[1]

This chapter will deal with the challenge that living with AIDS presents to the dualistic perspective from which many Christians approach life, a perspective embedded in our New Testament tradition. AIDS is at present a terminal disease. Thus, it poses many questions about God and life in the face of seeming hopelessness. It also presents the church with a crisis of self-understanding through the discovery of the barriers our perspectives erect to ministry and caring. By serious involvement in this struggle and with others involved in the AIDS crisis, some Christians are finding their understanding of faith, faithfulness, and community changing. The crisis of AIDS, then, calls on us to ask what it means to be faithful to Christ as Lord *in our time*; to seek to discern where God is acting within history *in our time*; and to go again to the well of our biblical tradition so as to draw from it those living waters that may nourish and inform.

This was my own experience as I sought to come to terms with the experience of AIDS through the study made by our group, a unit of the National Council of Churches' Faith and Order Commission, and within my own community of Bethlehem, Pennsylvania. Through my contacts with the Metropolitan Community Church, I found the presence of God in ministry to those suffering with AIDS in a community that, years ago, I could not have accepted as Christian. I had to deal with my own homophobia. Through my family experience, I had been acquainted with the tragedy of long-term illness, but this was something different and more massive. Since New Testament and spiritual formation are my disciplines, I found myself drawing on both to understand and to seek to be, with others, in my own small way, church. I find myself gradually willing to be a part of a church that has AIDS.

When confronted with crises that challenge assumptions and pose a paradigm change, we have several choices, among which are: to cling tenaciously to previous understandings or to remain open, willing to take the risk of seeing where God and circumstances will take us, and willing to understand in new ways.

The early church provides us with a helpful model in the way it came to terms with the inclusion of the Gentiles into a community that was originally Jewish and was under pressure from Jewish authorities to remain faithful to Jewish traditions. According to Luke's description in Acts, the church was forced to follow where God was going, and to include those whom God was including in a mission to Gentiles the church was not sure it wanted. Its reluctance is understandable, but the amazing thing is that it eventually came to terms with its new inclusive community, because it felt God had legitimized it.

LIVING WITH A LIVING GOD AND TRADITION

Paul's account in Galatians of his involvement in this process is worth treating in some detail. His conversion experience was a "revelation" that completely changed his previous opposition to the Christian movement (1:12–14). Though Paul does not share with us all the details of his struggle to come to terms with this experience, he is clear that his mission to the Gentiles arose from it (1:16). In 1:15, where Paul speaks of the God who "had set me apart before I was born," he alludes to the Old Testament's prophetic tradition by using words used by both Jeremiah and Isaiah. The context of these passages contains reference to a mission to Gentiles (see Isa. 49:1 and Jer. 1:5). It is then likely that Paul looked to scripture to understand both his experience and the newly developing Gentile mission, and saw those passages in the prophets in new ways and identified with them. His description of his first visit to Jerusalem includes nothing of the content of his discussions with church leaders, but the description of his second visit does. Paul presented to them his understanding of the gospel he preached among the Gentiles "lest somehow I should be running or had run in vain" (Gal. 2:2). The Jerusalem leaders agreed with him, for they perceived "the grace that was given"

(2:9). Peter and Barnabas's backsliding from relationship with Gentile Christians at Antioch (2:11ff.) probably precipitated a magnificent, extended theological treatise on Jewish Christian theology. Its perspective included the Gentiles as children of God in Christ, and completely reinterpreted Paul's previous paradigm of Jewish history and spiritual life.[2]

The Bible as a whole may be viewed as reflecting frequent paradigm shifts: it is a living, rather than a static tradition. The past action of God is continuously re-understood in the light of the present action of God and crises that call forth new insights. Both history and God cause the reshaping of the forms of faith. Much of the New Testament affirms this process by which the present activity of God (i.e., the Spirit) leads to truth (e.g., John 16:12–15). For the early church there were, among others, the crises of persecution, the inclusion of the Gentiles (already discussed), and the delay of the return of Christ.

THE IMPLICATIONS OF DUALISM

Dualism is the dividing of life and world into different and opposing elements rather than seeing them as a coherent whole. Historically, it has often meant seeing the world in terms of opposing forces: good and evil, spirit and flesh, God and Satan, God and world. Christianity has traditionally seen the world in this way because dualism is so embedded in the cultures that gave birth to the New Testament literature. One must grant that dualism is not only a cultural inheritance but also a serious attempt to explain the experience of human existence.

In our struggle to exist, we experience the destructiveness of the world and its seeming opposition to God, along with our struggles with our "flesh," and we can easily divide the world into good and bad. And yet the world, so fragmented and without an underlying unity, is not conducive to life and wholeness. On the contrary, Buddhism sees a basic unity underlying all existence (as does much of the Old Testament) and dualism as a creation of the human mind. In Christianity today there are those who are seriously challenging this dualistic perspective, such as Matthew Fox and his "creation spirituality" and Gerald May in his contemplative approach to psychology and spirituality.[3]

In response to the ministry of Jesus the church needs to be concerned about the ministry of healing and caring. If we listen to the parable of the last judgment in Matthew 25, we will ultimately be judged not only by how we cared for those like us, but for "the least of these" who were not openly identified with Jesus. On the other hand, we must learn from the healing action of outsiders, like the Samaritan, as discussed by Katharine Sakenfeld [ch. 12, pp. 179-180]. The church then, to be faithful, needs to explore how its perspectives stand as impediments to healing.

There are several ways in which dualism is a barrier to healing. One is the opposition of God and world. When Judaism and early Christianity saw the world as under the power of Satan, they were speaking a powerful truth: that the world often seems hostile to human existence. The experiences of this last century make this difficult to deny. And yet, along with our recognition that evil is a factor of human experience, if we only see the world as evil and human existence as tenuous and anxious, we predispose ourselves to illness through the continuous effects of stress. We become aliens in a strange and hostile world, separated from those elements in the world that would support our health and healing: our oneness with creation, with human community, and with the God who dwells within the paradox of creation and provides stability at the deepest levels of human existence.

Moreover, the God-world dualism causes spirituality to become separated from justice, and so healing is not seen in relationship to political and social context. The evil nature of the present age means that real change must wait for the coming kingdom of God, when God will destroy this world and create another in which God and justice will prevail. This apocalyptic hope for justice has lost faith in the possibility of justice in the present. It is striking that Jesus' message in Luke, announced in the sermon in the Nazareth synagogue (Luke 4:16–30), treats so many social issues. In the Lukan Beatitudes, Jesus pronounces blessing upon the poor, hungry, and weeping, with accompanying woes to the rich and satisfied. In contrast, in Matthew the Beatitudes are spiritualized to bless the poor in spirit and those who hunger and thirst for righteousness (compare Luke 6:20–26 and Matt. 5:3–12). Even the coming of the kingdom in the Matthean version of the Lord's Prayer is spiritualized by the addition of this interpretive line: "Thy will be done, on earth as it is in heaven" (compare Luke 11:2 and Matt. 6:10). Apocalyptic dualism is really a loss of faith in the possibility of the prophetic and the possibility of social change, caused by theological presuppositions and historical impotence. To find the spiritual, one must in that case look up to heaven or out to the end of history.

Another dualism is the opposition of flesh and spirit. Galatians 5:16–25 pretty well represents the New Testament attitude toward the fleshly human body. Nothing good comes out of the flesh, and it is opposed to the spiritual. "Flesh" also would include much of what we would speak of today as psychological.

To avoid this dualism is difficult, because we experience that the fleshly body often limits as well as facilitates life, and so at times seems to be over against us. It facilitates life when it works well; when we have a good golf game, when we speak well because our mind is clear and pain is minimal, or when our psyche is not too troubled. However, in illness, physical or psychological, we experience ourselves functioning through an organism which severely limits us, whose frailty endangers us, and whose pain dulls our senses.

Modern medical science has clearly indicated the biological mechanisms by which health is maintained and disease is combated. Whatever we believe about the soul's being the essence of the human and the body a temporary vehicle for it, *in the here and now* our existence is physical, fleshly, bodily. Thus if we reject the vehicle of our existence we also reject the possibilities of health, healing, and wholeness.

Our concern for healing then calls upon us to overcome the separation of self-spirit-soul from the body, and to look upon existence as embodied. In this way the healing mechanisms of the body are given their opportunity to function. This works both ways: it makes available to the soul-person the power of the body, and makes available to the body-person the power of the soul.

The opposition of good and bad is another type of dualism, though we do not often think of it in that way. I am in no way advocating a lack of moral principle by what I say. What I am concerned about is the tendency to label persons good or bad, or to label parts of ourselves as good or bad. Christianity has often degenerated into a sort of first-century pharisaism where the "bad" both within and outside of ourselves is to be separated off. For individuals, this means the repression and denial of parts of ourselves that belong to our humanity. Such parts might become redemptive and creative if integrated into the rest of our personalities, but when rejected they operate autonomously and below consciousness.

In the Christian community, this means that the community becomes the fellowship of the righteous rather than the fellowship of those seeking healing and wholeness within its love and support, and even those remaining within it need to hide their longing for healing because of the danger of rejection. This is particularly difficult because the homosexual community has been severely stricken with AIDS, and many Christian communities have tended to create community on the basis of their concept of sexual right(eous)ness rather than common humanity and the gospel's presentation of God's unconditioned love. Simplistic moral labeling, if such labeling is believed, cuts those so labeled off from the ground of their being and identity.

The consequences of dualism are clearly manifested in some of the stories included in Part Four. Hector was from a poor Puerto Rican family and had little early feeling for the church because "They didn't pay much attention to me." When he told his family he had AIDS, he was "kicked out of the house. I felt like a leper." The small evangelical church he attended rejected him because of his homosexuality. In a time of improving health, he identifies his improvement with God, and finds evidence that God really loves him, something he failed to find in the church. He concludes, "I don't trust the church. . . . Actually, I wonder if God isn't making me better because he wants *me* to start a church," a church in which those like him would have a place [ch. 10, pp. 152-153].

The name of the "Hidden Grievers," the support group in Patrick Cogan's description of a program at St. Vincent's Hospital in New York, describes the tragic hiddenness of the grief of so many who have lost a loved one to AIDS. Here one can hear the dualism of good and bad, of spirit and body (or sexuality), of God and world [ch. 10, pp. 161-162].

BIBLICAL MODELS FOR OVERCOMING DUALISM

Without carefully listening to the total message of the New Testament, one may hear only a dualism that separates Christians from the world and from others. One only has to think of the Johannine tradition. In spite of my fondness for it, I must confess that it is the most dualistic in the New Testament. The affirmation of the pre-incarnate Word's relationship to creation in the Prologue to the Gospel is found only here. The perspective contained in this borrowed piece is developed nowhere else in Johannine literature.[4] In Romans 9, Paul both transcends and uses the terminology of double predestination employed within some elements of Judaism: "vessels of mercy" and "vessels of wrath made for destruction."[5] In the Gospel of Matthew, Jesus, portrayed as a new Moses, calls for discipline in terms of his commandments, a righteousness greater than that of the scribes and Pharisees, perfection "as God is perfect."[6] Such a reading perpetuates the Pharisaic and Essene dualism of righteous and unrighteous, pure and impure, children of light and children of darkness.

The dualistic elements within the New Testament are in tension with other elements that lead in a different direction. These other elements supply the basic energy of the gospel. They are foundational to it and central to the ministry of Jesus. As the church struggles with the AIDS crisis and the self-understanding that is at the heart of this struggle, it needs to explore these themes.

First, there is the action of Jesus. Most of the form critics, whatever they may question on a historical basis within the gospel tradition, are struck by the persistence of the theme that Jesus did not draw social and religious limits where contemporary religious leaders did. In the parable of the prodigal son at the heart of the Gospel of Luke, the father refuses to draw a line between himself and his failed children.[7] Jesus' stories about Samaritans (the healed leper and the good Samaritan) pattern behavior through outsiders (Luke 10:25ff; 17:11ff.). Jesus announces in the Nazareth synagogue that his message is for the poor, the captives, the blind, and the oppressed (Luke 4:16ff.). And in the Lukan and Johannine traditions, women play roles that go beyond social stereotypes.

The cross, in a very special way, binds spirituality to the earth, for the proclamation of God's justice and mercy is no longer tied to the possibility of its historical realization. It is here that God declares openly both justice and mercy (Rom. 3:22b–26). Many in the early church, including the Corinthians and Luke in Acts, would rather have had a triumphal spirituality centered on the resurrection and the Spirit, and viewed the cross only as a historical tragedy. Paul and John both fought to keep the cross central, Paul by indicating that the cross opposed all human presuppositions and John by having the resurrected Jesus appear with his wounds (1 Cor. 1; John 21:19–29). The latter, preserved within a dualistic New Testament tradition, is an interesting example of the way these other elements stand in tension with dualism.

In the Pauline literature, one finds the theme that Christ overcomes all dividing walls to create a new unity. In Ephesians, Christ "has broken down the dividing wall of hostility" (2:14) that he might reconcile Jew and Greek in "one body" (2:16) and there is *one* body, *one* Spirit, *one* hope, *one* Lord, *one* faith, *one* baptism, *one* God. In Philippians, Paul rehearses the hymn of Christ's self-emptying as an exhortation to love and accord. In Colossians, he speaks of "the mystery hidden for ages and generations but now made manifest to [the] saints" (1:26), so that the riches of God's glory is for all. In language used of Jewish Wisdom, he speaks of all things being created through and for Christ, holding together in him whose purpose it is to reconcile all things. In Galatians, the giving of God's self, the Spirit, is the fulfillment of the promise given to Abraham and realized in Christ, and it enables all to utter, "Abba, Father," thus diminishing to insignificance all other identities: racial (Jew and Greek), economic (slave and free), and sexual and social (male and female) (Eph. 2:14–16; 4:4–6; Phil. 2:5–11; Col. 1:15–20, 26–27; Gal. 3:6–4:6).

Although the eschatology of the early church was by and large world-denying and understood the world as under the power of Satan and moved the unification of the cosmos into the future, in Paul the Spirit was understood as the present experience of the future. In John, eternal life was moved into the present, and the future paled in significance. Unfortunately, present realization was seen as occurring primarily within the Christian community. And yet there is great power within eschatology. There, hope and action can be directed toward the realization of the cosmos as God's kingdom. Caught between the tensions of the Christ-event and the future, the dynamics of human possibility and transformation are released, and even in the worst of Apocalyptic the call to God for justice is heard, echoing Jesus' proclamation of the kingdom.

This is not merely an essay. It describes a paradigm shift for me in responsibility to God and to our times, accompanied by insights into the biblical traditions. It is an attempt to be faithful. This journey has been facilitated by my community within the Faith and Order Commission, with which I have shared a common but multifaceted journey. Not all would agree with what I say here, but all would agree that we have tried together to be church.

6   *Susan E. Davies*

Oppression and Resurrection Faith

As a member of the National Council of Churches' Study Group on Unity and Renewal, I have received from Ron Russell-Coons and other members of the gay community a new and more profound understanding of Paul's ringing affirmation in Romans 8:38–39: "For I am sure that neither death, nor life, nor angels, nor principalities, nor things present, nor things to come, nor powers, nor height, nor depth, nor anything else in all creation, will be able to separate us from the love of God in Christ Jesus our Lord."

My intermittent encounters with AIDS, like those with the Holocaust before it, has framed life for me and given it shape; they wrench the focus away from the mundane, starkly spotlighting the fundamental connection between human integrity and salvation. In the process of action and reflection, I have come to see within the gay community a model of resurrection strength forged in death and oppression and based in community. This model profoundly challenges my understanding of the church as a people of the resurrection, for it highlights the contrast between our theology and our present practice. The author of "A Journey Toward Freedom" (chapter 3), speaking of life in the gay community in the face of AIDS, puts my new image very well:

90

[W]e live it all, the joy and the pain, as best we can—
fully, even voraciously, knowing that every moment,
joyful or painful, is a gift. On our worst days, we live in
fear. On our best, we live without it, because we have
named it and seen it and borne it together. We remember when we bore it alone, when . . . we couldn't even
say what "it" was. What we bear now is painful beyond
expression . . . because now it is the living pain of a
community learning to love itself, not the dead pain of
cultural and personal denial, and it is in the painful life
of our community that we now claim the joy of our
salvation.

Hope born of an encounter with death, loving community created in the midst of oppression and fear,
courage in the face of insidious attack, integrity and
solidarity growing from struggle—these are the
marks of the gay community as it lives with AIDS.
What are the marks of the church as it lives with
AIDS? Where is holiness or unity, universality or justice or apostolicity? How do our theology and our
present practice reflect the resurrection community
in the light of AIDS? The following pages explore
these questions, and propose a different mode of response for the church.

THE NATURE OF OPPRESSION

Oppression is the exercise of authority or power in
a burdensome, cruel, or unjust manner. Governments
are described as oppressive when they systematically
restrict and violate the civil and personal rights of
their citizens. Organizations and social systems are
oppressive when they suppress and deny the humanity of individuals simply because they fit certain
categories.

People with AIDS in our society are oppressed for
two reasons: because they have AIDS, and because the

majority of people with AIDS in the United States are members of oppressed groups before they contract AIDS.

A Defined Norm of Personhood

The oppression of any group, such as women; people of color; gay men and lesbians; the poor; the physically, mentally, or emotionally disabled; or the old, begins with a defined norm of personhood.[1] Such a norm is a standard, sometimes unspoken, that declares who is the most real, the most fully human, the most thoroughly acceptable kind of person in any given situation. Oppression has its origins in the use of that standard to judge all people and to enforce the exclusion or punishment of those who do not meet the standard. Those outside the standards are experienced as "other" by those who fit the norm, and treated as though they were less than fully human.

In our society, the defined norm, found in our language and laws, churches, synagogues, and mosques, businesses and schools and clubs, is white, male, youthful, temporarily able-bodied, heterosexual, educated, and Christian, with access to financial and economic resources.

This norm does not reflect the majority of people in our country or in any country. It does not reflect the majority of people in our churches or our schools. It certainly does not reflect the majority of people in our cities or suburbs, rural areas or reservations, factories and service industries; nor does it describe farmworkers, miners, secretaries, state employees, people in the food service, fishing, and lumbering industries, or people in real estate or human services. It does not reflect those who live in substandard housing, nor those who receive public assistance, or the 37 million of us who do not have health insurance.

The norm does, however, reflect the majority of people in Congress; in the courts; in public, business, and church leadership. It reflects those teaching in the universities and colleges; those who own land, buildings, and mines; those practicing medicine and ministry and law. It reflects the majority of those who occupy positions of power and prestige in our society.

The defined norm describes a small portion of our society, that which presently has power and authority. The possession of power leads to the second part of the nature of oppression.

Enforcement of the Norm

In order to be oppressive, the norm must be enforced by "institutional power, economic power and both institutional and individual violence."[2] Those who do not have institutional power may establish a norm for themselves and judge others by their ability to meet the defined norm. But unless they have the power to enforce their norm, they are merely bigots, not oppressors. Thus black people or women in our society may have individual or group prejudices against white people or men, but until either group has the power to enforce their prejudices through the legal, economic, and political system, we cannot call such prejudices reverse sexism or racism. We may only call them prejudice or bigotry.

At present, in the United States, AIDS is largely a disease of oppressed groups: gay men, black and Hispanic women and men, prostitutes, and intravenous drug users of every racial and ethnic background. These groups of people are oppressed because they do not fit the defined norm of personhood for our society, and because they are victims of institutional and economic power and both institutional and individual violence.

If we look at homophobia (the irrational fear of homosexual people), such institutional and economic power can be clearly seen. In most states, those who, merely on the basis of their sexual orientation, lose their jobs, or their children in a custody battle, are denied a mortgage, or harassed on the street, have no legal recourse. Gay and lesbian couples of long or short standing have no legal right to attend each other in the hospital or to request medical information about each other, may not benefit from each other's medical insurance, may lose their jointly held property at the death of the partner, and are not regarded as family for purposes of inheritance or taxes. They are often denied rental housing or public accommodation, and risk scorn or violence if they kiss each other good-bye in the car when they arrive at work or hold hands in public.

Both the law and the mores of our society insist that being gay or lesbian is sufficiently different from the norm as to be, in itself, demonstration of unfitness for employment, housing, parenting, or ordination. The individual's abilities, gifts, training, and experience are ignored in the face of one factor in their personal makeup.

Our local newspaper frequently prints verbal attacks on gay men and lesbian women, occasionally vehement claims that, in the words of a recent letter writer, "According to my Bible, those people do not have a right to live." In my community, five years ago a young gay man was killed by teenage boys who threw him off a bridge to drown after beating him. Several local members of the clergy said that the boys had been doing God's work in ridding the country of "those people." Oppression exists when the defined norm is enforced with personal and institutional violence.

THE NATURE OF AIDS

In the United States, AIDS is associated with homosexuality. In Africa, almost all those infected with the
AIDS virus are heterosexual. But in North America,
AIDS was first identified within the population of adult
gay men, and it retains its image as "the gay disease."

AIDS is a complex social phenomenon that connects
all of us with three terrifying realities: death, sexuality,
and otherness. AIDS is a disease that is transmitted
through the exchange of body fluids, either sexually or
by other means. It has as yet no known cure, although
researchers continually draw closer to treatments that
hold the symptoms in check. AIDS still largely affects
those who are experienced as other, as outside the defined norm, although it is rapidly spreading among
teenagers of all racial-ethnic and social groups.

In the last one hundred years, death has become for
us a frightening topic. The act of dying has been
moved from the home to the hospital or the nursing
facility, and power over it has been transferred from
the church to the hands of the medical professionals.
Most people have never actually helped anyone die.
Only in the last twenty years have some begun again to
say that a person has died, rather than "passed on" or
"been taken from us."

For two thousand years, the church has claimed that
death has lost its sting, that Christ is Lord both of life
and of death; and yet we have lived as though death
were an evil power that wreaks havoc where it will,
scything through our lives with bitter vengeance. We
are taught to regard death as punishment for sin, rather
than as part of the normal course of mortal human life, a
final step into eternal life in the presence of God.

Thus, when faced with a disease that as yet has no
cure, we are terrified. We burn children out of their

homes, we let persons with AIDS die on the streets of our cities, and we try to exclude them from the workplace. From some of our churches come thunderings about the wages of sin, and from some of our people, threats and acts of murder and abuse. AIDS faces us with our deepest fears about death.

The church has historically done an even less estimable job on questions of sexuality. The great doctors of the church have claimed that we are sexual beings because we are fallen, sinful beings and that, at best, we were given this great source of communication and pleasure merely for the procreation of the race. We are not comfortable with our nature as sexual beings. We do not speak of it in church meetings or in public worship. Sexual activity is, by and large, something that occurs in privacy, in the bedroom, and is not spoken of by decent people.

To be faced, then, with a disease identified as transmitted primarily by sexual activity is to have to face our own ambivalence and confusion about our own sexuality and sexual activity, as well as that of our children. And if the disease is also deadly, our shuddering terror rises to great heights.

Added to death and sexuality is this third ingredient: that the sexual activity in question is being engaged in by those who are experienced as thoroughly unacceptable in their personhood, by those who are other, whose very existence threatens the defined norm by which people are judged in our society and in our churches. The life story of Hector tells how he was rejected by his family and the pastor of his church because he was gay [ch. 10, p. 152]. He was rejected by hospitals in both New York City and Puerto Rico because he had AIDS. Ron Russell-Coons's letters trace his relationship with his family as they struggle with both his sexuality and his illness [ch. 2, p. 45]. To have AIDS in our society is to have "the gay disease," transmitted only by "perverted" sexual activity. Those who are "other" must bear not only the effects of the disease but the ostracism of their condemned sexuality.

AIDS is presently a disease of socially stigmatized groups. Those who have the disease but do not belong to these groups are called "innocent victims," people who, because of their class membership, do not seem to deserve AIDS: hemophiliacs, infants born to mothers with AIDS, the heterosexual spouse of a gay man or intravenous drug user, heterosexual teenagers, transfusion recipients.

Declaring one group guilty and another innocent provides categories of condemnation for those who do not fit the defined norm. Those who are other have been declared guilty in their essence as human beings, and, as the theological statement of the black Episcopalians argues, such a declaration provides an opportunity for invoking the wrath of God on those who are seen to deserve punishment [ch. 13, p. 187]. Medically, everyone is innocent. A virus attacks human beings when and where it can. It is no respecter of persons. Distinguishing between means of contracting the disease is a mechanism of oppression, and must be recognized as such, especially in the church.

A MODEL FROM THE GAY COMMUNITY

In response to this threefold threat of death, sexuality, and otherness, the overt and covert message of the church to those with AIDS has been to continue the oppressive dualism of our culture rather than acting on our resurrection faith. In far too many cases, the church has acted as though some deserve their suffering because of their lifestyle or social status, while others are seen as suffering innocently because of the evil deeds of more sinful people. The marks of the church have too often been fear and oppression rather than holiness and justice.

I propose an alternative model for our response, a model offered us directly by the gay community. It is a model based on integrity and compassion, one that insists on justice for all members of our society, and is derived from a deeper and clearer understanding of Romans 8.

AIDS has been and continues to be an agency of oppression. As is so clearly and painfully delineated by Randy Shilts in his powerful book *And the Band Played On*,[3] both official and unofficial response to AIDS from 1982 through 1986 was one of embarrassment and avoidance, of panic and the blaming of victims. Most of the church has continued in the same pattern.

The gay community, on the other hand, and those among it who have the disease, have insisted that the AIDS epidemic has been and can continue to be an occasion for human strength and dignity, compassion and action, anger and outrage in the face of oppression and death. AIDS has provoked and exposed bitter divisions within the community of gay and lesbian people. It has also been an extraordinary occasion for both political and interpersonal solidarity.

Many within the gay community are finding a more faithful way to respond to suffering, a model grounded in the truth of Romans 8, and one that can be seen clearly in Beryl Ingram-Ward's experience of a space for hospitality and hope [ch. 4, p. 69]. The model has its roots in the experiences of oppressed people throughout the world. It is a model offered by African-American slave rebellions in the United States, by the development of basic Christian communities within the Roman Catholic Church in Latin America, by the antiapartheid movement in South Africa, and by resistance movements throughout history. It is simply that the freedom to act and live in the face of oppression and death is found in the certainty that nothing can separate us from our own integrity and solidarity.

Paul declared that nothing could separate us from the love of God in Jesus Christ. For Christians within and outside the gay community, the depth of this truth is coming alive in their agonizing struggle with AIDS. For others, who do not claim Christian faith, the experience takes on different words but has a remarkably similar outcome. Michael Callen, who had lived with AIDS for six and a half years when he spoke in Augusta, Maine, in November, 1988, used these words:

> The mind needs to tell the body to fight—that life is precious and worth living. The mind is a great, largely untapped pharmacy and we've got to find creative ways to mine it. Joy juice is what the body needs to live. And hope is like the air that we breathe; without it, we wither and die. . . . I'm happier now than at any other point in my life. AIDS was kind of a cosmic kick in the ass for me. It made me realize the preciousness of life. It made me face hard questions and make some difficult choices. . . . I viewed my life as a rehearsal awaiting that all-important performance which never came. But AIDS shook most of that out of me. The shock of diagnosis did more for me than 10 years of therapy ever could. . . . Though I would not have wanted a catalyst as catastrophic as AIDS, I am a changed man. And being happy helps fuel my will to live.[4]

After the shattering readjustment and agony brought by an AIDS diagnosis, strength and courage have come to the gay community as a whole, and to many individuals with AIDS within that community as well as to their loved ones. They have refused to become or remain victims. They have retained or gained personal agency, and acted with a freedom and honesty which, for

many, had not been possible before that time. In Ron
Russell-Coons's words (see chapter 1),

> So we are learning to live in joy. We are learning about
> liberation. We can't really be free until we have en-
> tered the struggle. The dawn of my liberation—my
> personal liberation—is finally coming. I have spent a
> lifetime wrestling with the angel of struggle. I have
> been freed and sent on with a blessing. We are also
> learning about peace in the midst of our fears. Our an-
> ger *can* be transformational. We discover that compas-
> sion knows no color, gender, age, or lifestyle. Our
> humanity makes us one. In all this, we are learning
> more about the resurrection.

The gay community and the persons with AIDS
within it continue to suffer both physically and psychi-
cally. Their medical bills continue to stagger them, and
their insurance is still canceled. Their strength is
sapped, and emotional challenges continue to devas-
tate. But, withal, a freedom is being dearly bought. An
integrity has been and is being painfully achieved.
They have created a community in which they experience themselves as strong, valued, full human beings.
They will no longer accept the defined norm that ex-
cludes them. They know that nothing can separate
them from their own integrity and solidarity, and that
they are free to act and to be without fear of cultural
enforcement or religious condemnation.

RESURRECTION FAITH AND THE CHURCH

This freedom, this integrity so painfully purchased,
is like nothing so much as the resurrection life of which
Christians sing. We claim a resurrection faith. We
claim the glories of a life of fullness and wholeness, of
strength and dignity, and we read scriptures that grew
out of communities whose experience was much closer

to that of today's gay communities than to the mainstream of American society.

The freedom which is ours in Christ is precisely the freedom to act and to be in a way which can no longer be controlled by force or enforcement, by cultural imperatives or social stigma. It is a freedom which derives from the certainty that nothing can separate us from the love of God—not death, not otherness, not oppression, not AIDS.

In response to the AIDS crisis, large parts of the gay community have found a new way of acting, a new model for life. They have grounded themselves in a bedrock integrity, a certainty that they are free to act and to live in the face of oppression and death, that nothing can separate them from their own intrinsic worth as human beings. They will no longer accept a definition of themselves as lesser, as other, as sinful, as not fully human. They have received into their own hands the right to experience themselves as full, valid, functioning, loving, strong human beings. And, as they have struggled to this insistence in the face of oppression from the church as well as the rest of society, they offer to the church a model of strength, courage, and compassion.

It is a model with very old roots, growing from the same stock as resurrection faith, stretching through resistance movements throughout history: the defeat of the powers of death and evil, the defeat of the powers of oppression.

Seeing this model in the gay community challenges me to look again at the church's claim to be a resurrection community. What is at stake in our response to AIDS is our very life as the church, as those who claim faith in the power and the presence of God to overcome evil and death. The experience of the gay community in living with AIDS has shed light on Romans 8 for me and for the church. Their experience calls forth, as a matter of justice, the embodiment of the resurrection faith we claim in Christ. We are called to change the marks we exhibit from fear and oppression to holiness and justice. We are called, by Christ and by the gay community, to live in that freedom we are given, certain that nothing can separate us from the love of God—not death, not otherness, not oppression, not AIDS.

Such change cannot occur within the church without struggle, without wrenching self-examination, just as it did not come to the gay community without a fierce and ongoing confrontation with oppression and death. Were the church to live with justice in the context of AIDS, it would mean an end to our condemnation of those whom we have heretofore defined as less than fully human. It would mean a recognition of the full personhood of gay men and lesbian women as people created by and beloved of God, not in spite of their "sin," but because of their inherent worth as full members of the human race. With respect to the AIDS epidemic, it would mean taking upon ourselves the responsibility not only for the oppression we have fostered, but also for providing personal, medical, and financial support for those who are suffering with AIDS, and doing so with as much energy and dedication as we have given to those who are old, or to children maimed by disease.

It would mean confessing the sin of which we are guilty, that of distorting the relationship between ourselves and others; specifically, members of the gay community. We have based that relationship on our power to determine who is acceptable in the eyes of the law, the church, and God. In so doing, we have become oppressors, and have strayed from the values of justice and peace which are at the foundation of God's good creation.[5]

We who are the church are already suffering with
AIDS. Our members have AIDS. The families and friends
of those who have AIDS are church members. Our very
integrity as a people of the resurrection is at stake in
the way we respond to having AIDS. We are called to
follow that model of integrity and resistance to oppression offered us by the gay community, as we follow the
way of the one who came that all might have life, and
life more abundantly.

PART THREE

Signs of the Church

What does it take for the church to be a church that makes a difference for persons with AIDS? If we can find some clues to what it means to be the church with AIDS, we might come to a clearer understanding of the nature and mission of the church in a world of crisis. This in turn might help the church to be a sign of God's new creation as it moves toward wholeness, healing, and justice in the face of suffering and oppression. Self-understanding and renewal may be a gift of the Spirit as we participate in God's mission of setting free the groaning creation in all its parts. Searching for signs of the church in the context of the struggle with AIDS may contribute to other ecclesiologies by providing clues to renewal in the midst of crisis.

Our reflections on what it means to be a church are part of a worldwide study made by the World Council of Churches, "The Unity of the Church and the Renewal of Human Community."[1] Responding to the initiative of the Faith and Order Commission of the WCC, our study group in the United States began a study of points where a theology of life is emerging from situations of struggle, and where ecclesiology is changing in response to the situations of groaning, struggle, and death (see Preface). Using a "theology of engagement," we sought out situations where Christians were seeking to witness in situations of crisis and injustice, and we tried to understand what it would mean to be the church in these places of struggle. The first round of reflection is represented in chapter 7, by Marjorie Suchocki, and chapter 8, by Robert Schreiter. This round also includes a case study from the UFMCC Faith, Fellowship, and Order commission, titled "AIDS, Homophobia, and the Church."[2]

In the second round of reflection on case materials drawn from communities of faith and struggle, the Study Group on Unity and Renewal decided to test their growing insights into the nature of the church at one of the most difficult break-points of contemporary life: living with AIDS. Again, the group worked to develop firsthand knowledge of the challenges, pain, and insights of those working directly in the struggle with AIDS, and then to reflect on what we were learning about the nature of the church. In this process of ecumenical searching for unity and renewal, we were developing a new approach to the discussion of unity.

For many years, the ecumenical movement has sought unity of doctrine and church order through a discussion of convergence and divergence in doctrines and church order between confessional groups.[3] Recently, studies such as the one on unity and renewal have also included a contextual methodology; or, moving from action in concrete situations to the discussion of doctrine. This search for clues to ecclesiology includes both these methods, but moves one step further by placing a great deal of emphasis on unity through shared process and dialogue. In a sense this could be called a communal method of search for unity. The group works together, grows together, and shares that experience together with others (see Part Two).

All three chapters in this section on signs of the

church show what it takes for the church to be the church in the crisis of AIDS. Using the experience of those struggling with AIDS as a basis, they question church tradition and take a new look at the self-understanding of the church as one, holy, catholic, and apostolic. Marjorie Suchocki approaches this from the point of view of holiness and a renewed church, while Robert Schreiter examines all four signs in the light of the research of the Unity and Renewal study group. In "A Church for Troubled Waters" Letty Russell advocates the importance of the sign of justice as a crucial part of word and sacrament in the Christian church. Much more work is needed, and many more rounds of reflection are needed, but these chapters are an invitation to continue the same spiral process in the search for signs of unity and renewal in the church and in human community.

7 *Marjorie Suchocki*

Holiness and a Renewed Church

Brett called me from San Francisco, as he so often had; and as one so often does, I followed my pleased "Hello" with, "How are you?"

"Oh," he answered vaguely, "we'll talk about that later," and changed the subject. I followed his conversational lead, but my heart went heavy: Brett! Oh, please, God, not Brett! But, yes, Brett: slender, wistful, going-to-be-a-writer young Brett had AIDS.

So my sporadic letter-writing style underwent a radical change, and our correspondence became a regular keeping-in-touch. I felt the anguish of the compression of his dreams from a lifetime that had stretched over years to a lifetime touched by its imminent end. A brilliance came with that compression, like a diamond formed through the pressure of infinite time turned into infinite density. Little more than a year after that February phone call, the envelope was not from Brett, but from a stranger. It held two compact disks of Bach's music, with the single line, "Brett wanted you to have these." Oh, Brett!

How does the church respond to a tragedy that the church itself has compounded? For the tragedy is not only the physical reality of AIDS, but also the strong connection in America between AIDS and gay men like

Brett, coupled with the spiritual rejection of such persons in the depths of their personhood. The church's contributions to the marginalization and persecution of gays heighten the isolation caused by the disease and hinder the church from becoming a loving presence to those who suffer in their struggles to live with AIDS. This article suggests two responses, one involving a recovery of the church's story concerning our call to holiness, and the second involving our transformation through confession. As a church living through God's call to holiness, we must be present to, for, and with persons with AIDS, and we must radically reverse our participation in the ill-being of persons whose sexual orientation is toward those of their own gender.

RECOVERING THE CHURCH'S STORY

"Holiness" is not a word found often on the lips of mainline Christians. Sometimes we behave as if the word were a bit unseemly, belonging to saints of the past, or to some heaven of the future, or perhaps to some group we dismiss as "fringe" or "fanatic" in the present. Holiness is simply not a word we feel comfortable about applying to ourselves.

Yet through two thousand years the church has dared to recite a creed in which we apply the word "holiness" to the church, and theologians dealing in doctrines of the church inevitably wrestle with defining just what it means to describe this concrete church in our midst with the daunting word "holiness." I myself have become particularly intrigued with John Wesley's understanding of holiness as presented in his small classic, *A Plain Account of Christian Perfection*.[1] Recounting his doctrine in story fashion may convey to us more powerfully than the abstractions of systematic theology the pressing power of what it means to say that we are called by God to lives of holiness, or "Christian perfection."

God created the world for the sake of the holiness that would be made possible through Christ Jesus. This conviction threads its way through the story of holiness, like the leitmotif of a great and grand symphony: God creates the world in order that it might be holy, reflecting the glory of God's own self. In the far reaches beyond time, in the depths of God's own mystery, God stirred Godself to creation. And what would this creation be, this somethingness that God would call out of the chaos of nothingness? What pattern could exist, when nothing existed outside of God's eternity? Would God need a pattern at all? And the answer, of course, is "no": God created out of God's own goodness, which is to say, out of God's own generous love, or holiness. There was no pattern external to God, no eternal ideas hung like stars in an unending sky of nothingness! There was only God.

But if there is no pattern external to God, is not God's own self the pattern? "Let us create [humankind] in our image," is the Genesis word (1:26). A blue-green globe of earth is spun into space, whirling in place; by God's word its waters part and land is formed; by God's word its forests grow, its fish swim, its birds fly, and its animals roam in their appointed realms, all listening for God's culminating word: "Let us create [humankind] in our image"! Male and female God has created us, together to bear the divine image.

What could this image be? Like many theologians before and after him, Wesley connected the image of God with the rational abilities of humankind—not in a discursive mode, but in an intuitive awareness of the fundamental nature of all existence; its interconnectedness, and its relationship to God. The perfection of this awareness was not knowledge alone, but the responsive

and responsible orientation of one's whole being toward
love, which is the glory of God. Facilitating this orientation of one's being toward love was an original perfection of all one's powers of existence. Through love, the
created order would achieve its spiritual perfection in
an organic, interconnected unity.

Finally, then, in a Wesleyan theology, it is love as
well as reason that forms the image of God in creation.
Reason is for the sake of love. Where reason makes
distinctions, love creates unity. Just as the creative
God is a triune complexity where distinctions within
the Godhead are one in the deepest union of love,
even so the image of God in the finite order is distinctions, or diversity, existing in the interpenetrating
unity of love. The finite order glorifies God when its
teeming diversity is unified through love. Humankind,
as the agents of this love, are the unique bearers of
God's image, responsible for exercising love toward all
creation. Through the generosity and expansiveness of
love exercised throughout the whole created order,
the created order becomes *whole*, woven into a diverse
unity akin to God's own being. The ultimate image of
God is not rationality alone, but rationality in the service of love.

Wesley tells the tale of tragedy, wherein through
disobedience sin entered the world. Ultimately, disobedience is not a failure of reason but a failure to
love. The failure of love toward God is at the same time
a breakdown in the ability to fulfill the divinely appointed task of unifying the creation itself through
love. Unlove, unconnectedness, alienation, and separation all follow from the failure to love. The world,
created for the holiness that is love, falls into the frag-
mentation of unlove.

The story of redemption is the renewed offer of the
ability to love and therefore to carry out God's intent

for creation. Wesley traces the tale through successive means of inducing humankind toward the work of love: following the law of works in Adam, there is the three-fold law given through Moses, designed to channel human action into the ways of love. Political, cultic, and ceremonial laws, Wesley said, speak to all aspects of human existence, and, if followed, would ensure the flow of love. But what humankind would not do of its own will it cannot do through law, and the law became but an empty reminder of that which humankind failed to do. Therefore, God's own self entered into the story through incarnation: what we could not do, God would do for us. Jesus is at once the living manifestation of God's love for us and what our love should be toward one another. He broke the barriers of unlove that had been created through social restrictions and ostracism; he reached across the pyschic distance of human rejection to touch others with healing. Having manifested God's love in his life, he offered God's love through his death and resurrection. He himself drew into his own being all the consequences of unlove: its hatred, its rejection, its cruelty, its murderous effects. Just as he had manifested love in his life, he manifested the effects of unlove in his death. Drawing these all into himself, he died love's death. But the mystery is that the love of God is stronger than all our deaths, and so God raised him from the dead for our salvation.

What is salvation in the context of this story? Salvation is the re-creation of the possibility of humankind's fulfilling its created destiny; it is the renewed possibility of human love's being exercised toward God and the human community, spilling over into the entire created order so that all might manifest the complex unity of love in the image of God. In and through Jesus Christ, God offers the renewed creation of the world. God created the world for the sake of the holiness, or love, that is again made available through Jesus Christ.

Therefore, those who are in Christ are those who are called to, and empowered for, the renewal of love. The peculiarly Wesleyan twist to the story is the conviction that God's creative will need not be thwarted; it is possible, in this life, to live the love that God makes available for us in Christ. It is not simply possible, it is expected. Christians are called to the exercise of love, and this love is to be an overflowing care toward the well-being of all creation. This is our destiny. The story of creation continues as those who are renewed in Christ go about the work and works of love, empowered by the grace of God, striving toward the fullness of the created order. By God's grace, our interconnected and interconnecting works of love will be drawn into God's own creative love, and woven there into the ultimate destiny of the world, which is simply the world's perfection in love, in the fullness of the divine image.

Such are the contours of the cosmic story. Within our tiny times, we who live the church's story are to draw upon the strength and grace of God's own love and contribute the fullness of our powers toward the well-being of all the earth. In imitation of Christ, we are to break all barriers of social rejection and ostracism, and to see into the wonder of God's diverse creation. Through personal and societal modes of love, we are called to contribute to earth's reflection of the divine image, to the glory of God. As the church of Jesus Christ, we live from his love, manifesting it in our own personal and corporate witness.

THE IMPLICATIONS OF THE STORY

Wesley's doctrine of holiness has often been misinterpreted as a sort of superhuman mode of existence, where one never errs or makes mistakes of judgment, or gives in to human frailty. But Wesley's account makes no such claims; to the contrary, it states that "at present no [one] can at all times apprehend clearly, or judge truly. And where either the judgment or apprehension is wrong, it is impossible to reason justly. Therefore, it is as natural [to make a mistake] as to breathe; and [one] can no more live without the one than without the other" (CP 70). Using the paradigm of Adam and the universally fallen condition of humanity, he assumes that we are quite prone to error and to the vicissitudes belonging to our finite condition, but that such things need not be a hindrance to holiness. Holiness does not require a transcendence of our human condition, but a full utilization of our condition toward the concrete reality of love. In such a vision, justification is but a necessary prelude to the full drama of Christian perfection, or holiness. Holiness is not a release from finitude, but the orientation of all our finite powers, hindered though they be, toward love.

If the story told thus far centers on personal holiness, this is only because the assumed context is social holiness. Social holiness is that characteristic whereby the church as a whole is called on to manifest forms of love. Just as there are interpersonal forms of love appropriate to the individual, so there are also structural forms of love appropriate to institutions. The two forms are interwoven, of course, since individuals constitute institutions, and institutions shape individuals. To focus on one to the exclusion of the other is to distort the full requirement of love. While we are accustomed to descriptions of love as exercised by individuals, we are not so sensitive to institutional love.

An institution that is called to manifest the holiness of love must first exercise a constant critique of its own internal structures, measuring them according to the norm of love. This criterion necessarily becomes the welfare of those deemed by many to be "least." Contemporary liberation theology calls this "God's preferential option for the poor," continuing the sense in which the justice of ancient Israelite society was tested against the norm of those typically unprotected in society: the widow, the orphan, the stranger. The church, called to the holiness of love, must continuously ask itself if there are those within its own borders who are marginalized, pushed toward ill-being, by the church's institutional structure. To the degree that the answer is "yes," then the internal mission of the church is defined: it must restructure itself according to the inclusive norm of love. The church *qua* institution is holy insofar as its structures ensure the well-being of all its members; its structures must mediate a fullness of well-being throughout the institution. To the question, Who determines well-being? the answer must always fall with the "preferential option for the poor." Are there those within the church who cry out that the institutional structure mediates the impoverishment that is ill-being? Then the church, in responsive holiness, will examine and transform itself from that perspective. Its institutional structures must be as tough and as pliable as love; holiness means that the institutional structure of the church exists as channels of self-transforming love, in the image and glory of God.

But the nature of holiness is that it cannot be contained by borders. The church that is holy is holding not only its own institutional structures up to the transforming critique of love, but that church judges the structures of the wider society within which it exists against this same norm. The mission of the church beyond its borders must be to bring the critique of love to the social structures of its day. To what extent do the economic practices, the cultural suppositions, and the

political choices of a society contribute to or depend
on the ill-being of a people, whether within or beyond
the borders of the society? To that extent, the church
that lives by the holiness of God must announce a prophetic judgment, and bring its own structural powers
to bear upon the transformation of the wider society of
which it too is a part. Errors will be made, of course;
and here Wesley's injunction to the individual that holiness does not mean a perfection of reason or judgment is appropriate to the wider society as well. This
means that the church cannot call for social reforms in
a spirit of self-righteousness; rather, the church must
call for reforms as a participant in the problem, and as
one who by God's grace is putting its own house in
order, even as it calls on society to do likewise. The
church calls for structures that reflect love in the spirit
of love.

The intent of holiness is to weave all of creation together in the bond of love. The church is therefore
called as an agent of openness, an agent whose care
affirms different organizations, different structures, different societies, and different modes of being, so long
as they work toward the well-being of an increasingly
inclusive community. The ultimate model is the trinitarian God seen through Jesus Christ: a God whose
very being is irreducible diversity united in deepest
union: love. The church, imbued with such a model,
does not seek to conform all the world to its own way
of being; instead, it seeks to model the depths of diversity-in-unity within its own structures, and to call to
the wider society to do likewise. Like the ever-increas-
ing rings of the pebble in the pond, well-being is to
extend in increasingly wider circles until it embraces
the rich and teeming diversity of the whole created
order.

Always, the judgment of the church and of society is

the question of those who are deprived of well-being. How is it with the "least"? To the extent that there *are* those who can be named least, there is ill-being, and a failure of love. The church, called to holiness, is called to be transformatively present not only with interpersonal love but with the power of structures that mediate well-being, which is love, which is holiness.

Living the Church's Story

To tell the tale is fairly simple; to live the tale is another matter. We are called by a vision of holiness, and promised the grace of God toward our power of loving. Our failures are such that we are tempted to deny the very vision given us through Christ, or, if we hold to it nonetheless, to excuse our failures by relegating the call to a post-historical existence.

But there is a better way. We have at times been called a "confessing" church, meaning that we confess our faith even at the cost of martyrdom. Holiness adds a different nuance to our way of being a confessing church, which is simply to name our sins of unloving before God. In the naming, there is transformation, for to name our unlove is already to begin the gracious movement beyond it. Our particularity as a people of God is that we always are called to exist in the tension of a radical call to love, and a realization of the partiality of our love. The response to that tension cannot be despair, but must instead be an openness to God's call to the continual renewal of the church. The empowering grace of God is our source of hope, leading us always to confession and transformation and confession yet again. Throughout, we are borne up by the continuous love of God toward us. From God's love, we are empowered to live God's love.

This, of course, brings us to the contemporary issue

of persons living with AIDS, who are often those named
"least" in today's society. While this condition is by no
means confined to those who are gay, and threatens to
pervade all levels of society here in the United States
just as it does in several other countries, the problem
in our culture is inextricably bound up with the whole
issue of homosexuality. The church's deep ambiguity
concerning sexuality itself has only been compounded
when sexuality involves an orientation toward persons
of one's own gender, and the response of the church
has been to marginalize such persons under the rationale that they are sinners.

Such a rationale is certainly peculiar, given the reality that "sinner" is a category that our consciousness of
holiness and our weekly prayers of confession apply to
us all. We all know ourselves to be sinners who are
called and empowered for deeper modes of loving;
how, then, can naming another as "sinner" be rationale for exclusion? We are all those who, like Zac-
chaeus of the biblical text, receive the gracious
presence of God before we ask for it. Inclusion, not
exclusion, is the way of grace. Thus the shunning and
marginalization of persons whose sexual orientation is
toward their own gender can never be "justified" on
the basis that such persons, like ourselves, might be
sinners! Furthermore, sinning is not tied up with one's
sexual orientation, but with a failure to love, resulting
in actions that stem from the desire for the ill-being of
the other. It would appear in this case that it is the
church, not the differently oriented person, who is sinner, and the church who is called first to confession.

Confession leads to transformation in both personal
and societal modes of being. To name one's sin of unlove is already to begin the process of moving beyond
it; therefore, confession is itself a gracious act that
leads to the empowerment to love. Since our sinning is

both personal and corporate, so our confession must also be both personal and corporate as the church. We are called to release ourselves and our failures to the triune God, and open ourselves for God's faithful healing in return. Confession becomes the intent to release unlove, and to be open for God's fullness of love. Confession is therefore a gracious channel whereby God can yet call creation to become a manifestation of the divine image. It will inevitably lead toward our critical restructuring of our corporate mode of being toward a greater inclusiveness of well-being. Returning to the story of creation, we are mindful that the wonder of God's creation is the sense in which it embodies enormous diversity, and the culmination of creation is the unifying of all diversity through the weaving work of love. God's own self is already a diversity-in-unity as trinity, wherein the Creator God is an irreducible diversity bound together in deepest unity. The love within God does not obliterate the divine distinctions; rather, it brings them in to brilliant focus. The earth, as the image of God, is not called to subjugate differences to the imagined good of an absolute uniformity of being. Rather, we are called to celebrate differences in the unity of love. Love, not sameness, is the norm. Love seeks the well-being of all, and only those differences that are the work of unlove are called to judgment and transformation.

Is it not the case that, because AIDS in our country has taken an inordinate toll on the gay community, we have associated the disease with sexual orientation? The disease, then, has become the occasion for those who fear homosexuality to decry still further those who are already marginalized for their sexual orientation. We have taken the "poor" and, in their illness, made them poorer still. But if holiness calls us to examine our personal and institutional structures from the point of view of those who are marginalized by personal and social structures, then holiness calls us to confess our sins and enter transformatively into presence with and for the poorest of the poor, those struggling in life with AIDS.

The church is called to be holy and graced by the power of God to live in the risk of holiness. But holiness calls us to be open to our own transformation by the power of God and by the norm of God's love. Holiness demands the continuous renewal of the church, and the dynamic power of God's Spirit empowers this renewal; it makes it possible. Our own openness and assent make holiness actual, drawing upon God's grace to be the moving image of the triune God in our histories.

All holiness and acts of holiness are the many forms of love, and ultimately find their fullness in the love of God for us, and us for God. As we have had occasion to draw on a Wesleyan vision throughout this chapter, it is fitting to cite a description of the connection between our love for God and neighbor. "One of the principal rules of religion is, to lose no occasion of serving God. And since [God] is invisible to our eyes, we are to serve [God] in our neighbor, which [God] receives as if done to [Godself] in person, standing visibly before us" (CP 103). How does the church love God, and so exhibit holiness, in these times? We do so by standing with those who suffer, embracing them with inclusive love, and by questioning our institutional structures in openness to transformation according to the norm of love. In such ways we participate in the love of God, and move with the renewal of holiness.

8   *Robert J. Schreiter*

Marks of the Church in Times of Transformation

Reflection on whether there are specific defining characteristics of the church of Christ that are clearly evident to all is of ancient origin. Discussion of such characteristics usually begins with the words added to the Nicene Creed by the Council of Constantinople in 381: "[and in] one holy catholic and apostolic church."

Up to the time of the Reformation, there was little systematic reflection on these four "marks" or characteristics. Optatus and Augustine invoke them against the Donatists, and they show up in reflection on the church from time to time. The controversies around John Wycliffe and John Hus revived interest in them. But it was the Reformation that brought about the most reflection on them.

It is not the purpose of this chapter to recount that history; that can be found elsewhere.[1] But a number of points emerge from that history that are of importance for us here.

1. Reflection on the marks of the church has been at its keenest in times of change—changes that challenged the self-understanding of the church. Conflicts around Donatus in the early church, around Wycliffe and Hus in the medieval church, and between Catholics and Protestants in the sixteenth and seven-

teenth centuries, and among the Tractarians in the Church of England in the nineteenth century—all brought forth new and often complex thinking about the identity of the true church and how that identity might be ascertained.

It is not surprising, then, that the Unity and Renewal study group turned to a reflection on the marks of the church. The group had been concerned with conflictual situations in the human community and what the church meant in the midst of them. Reflection on the marks of the church has generally not been particularly lively in the twentieth century, perhaps because conflictual situations either have not been central or have been avoided by those engaging in the reflection. Adopting a reflection on the marks, however, can lead to a deepened understanding of the meaning of the church today.

2. Reflection on the marks of the church has generally occurred in situations of intrachurch conflict; that is, between competing bodies within the one church, each claiming to be the true manifestation of the church of Christ. This is especially clear in the Donatist and Reformation controversies. But even though they were used in this fashion, theologians (especially those on the Roman Catholic side) insisted upon their empirical, public, and verifiable nature—the marks were there for all rational beings to see and judge. The implication was that the marks had meaning beyond settling disputes within the divided body of Christ.

This implication was of special importance for the Unity and Renewal study. The marks have implications for intrachurch conflicts (as, for example, between the "official" and the "popular" church in Latin America), but also for discussing a perspective from outside the church into the church. Are there characteristics that help the nonbeliever recognize the church of Christ?

The reactions of many PWAs to their denominational churches reflect this kind of outsider perspective; they found themselves marginalized by both society and church. What kind of church did they find relating to them? How did those churches who call themselves Christian relate to PWAs?

3. Since at least the sixteenth century, the marks were construed in such a way that one could proceed deductively from the marks to the discovery of the true church. The very word used, *notae*, implied this: a move from the known to the unknown.

The WCC Unity and Renewal study's commitment to contextual and inductive methodologies would seem to run counter to this tradition. One might even ask why, today, one would turn to the *via notarum* as a way of examining the church at all. What became evident is that one can use a methodology of marks of the church in ways other than deductively, by initiating a dialogue that creates both a challenge to our understanding of the marks and a fresh reading of the conflictual situation.

4. There has been no consistent agreement in history on either the number or the nature of the marks. The four (one, holy, catholic, and apostolic) have only achieved widespread consensus since the beginning of the nineteenth century. Aquinas had four: unity, holiness, catholicity, and tenacity (*firmitas*) in faith. Luther had two: the gospel purely preached and the sacraments rightly administered. Counter-Reformation apologist Robert Bellarmine had fifteen, a number that remained influential in Roman Catholic circles for nearly three centuries. The Roman theologians Bovio and Lucchesini (in the sixteenth and seventeenth centuries, respectively) had one hundred!

The possibility of suggesting more, fewer, or other marks is therefore neither surprising nor innovative.

For most of the church's history, there has been no agreement on the marks, although some preference has been given to the Constantinopolitan four. Many have noted that the larger numbers are generally reducible to four.

5. There has been no consistent terminology for what are called here "marks." *Notae, signa, conditiones,* and *proprietates* have all been used, and all have different nuances of meaning. They also represent different levels of certitude, both about the identifiability of the marks and the exactitude of a methodology of applying them. Generally speaking, today there would be a great deal more modesty about a method using marks to unmistakably identify the true church of Christ than would have been the case a century ago.

Given the tentative and often tenuous nature of situations on the margins of society that we investigated, a "weaker" sense was preferred. Marks of the church only point to the reality of the church; they do not define and locate it.

The Methodology of the Unity and Renewal Study

As has been documented elsewhere, the Unity and Renewal study, both in its predecessor studies and in its transformations since 1968, has been concerned with the relation of the unity and identity of the church to the unity and redemption of the entire human community.[2] It was felt that something along that frontier could illuminate the nature of the church in a way that a study of its history or an intrachurch dialogue could not. It has also been recognized that traditional historical methodologies and modes of academic argumentation do not always capture the realities at work here. Consequently, there has been concern for a more empirical mode of operation, emphasizing context alongside content, and the particular in its own integrity rather than as an instance of the universal. Experiences in small Christian communities in Latin America and feminist circles in North America and Europe have contributed to this.

The Unity and Renewal study on AIDS turned especially to life stories to capture this empirical reality. These stories were sought out from the margins of the official church, where the church was not responding adequately to the AIDS crisis. By looking at those situations, we sought what Michel de Certeau called the *ruptures instauratrices*, those points of breakdown that have the potential of becoming sources of creativity rather than simply destruction. Some of that material can be found in the first and fourth part of this book.

This more empirical methodology, however, is not always easily defined or grasped. This is especially so when the official, organized church seems to be absent from the scene (as in the "No Name" story that Ron Russell-Coons presents in chapter 10). At that point, we sought "ecclesial clues," on a more intuitive basis. Ecclesial clues seem to be close to what traditionally were called *signa*, or signs of the church—those things that, rather than define or locate, point beyond themselves.

These emphases on the inductive and the provisional echo with what seems to be surfacing elsewhere in similar studies; namely, that the Unity and Renewal study helps focus on the eschatological nature of the church. Rather than emphasizing the future at the expense of the present, these studies show how that future is already manifesting itself in the present, as the appearance of life-giving realities in the face of death-dealing situations. This was especially evident in the AIDS case study presented by Jennie Boyd Bull,[3] and in the discussions of the difference between healing and being cured by Ron Russell-Coons and others (chapters 1 and 2).

To summarize, then, this investigation of the marks of the church took the form of discerning what the AIDS crisis has said to us about the meaning and shape of the church. Letty Russell explores this in more detail in the next chapter. The marks did not provide a template that could be fitted over any situation to discern the relative authenticity of the manifestation of the church of Christ. True, rather, to the underlying assumptions of an inductive and contextual methodology, it provided a road map in a continuing journey, always reminding us that the map is not the territory itself. The method implies a greater sensitivity to concrete and particular cases, and to what AIDS can teach us about a new, hoped-for wholeness in the world.

With that, we can turn to the results of our reflections on the marks of the church. Each section begins with a brief summary of consensus understandings from the wider church community,[4] followed by some things we learned in the life stories and case studies.

REFLECTIONS ON THE MARKS

One Church

Unity is considered by many to be the prime mark of the church of Christ, within which all the other marks find their origin. The unity of the church derives from the unity of the Godhead, and best mirrors the divine image in its unity. It also bespeaks the reunion of God and humanity in the justifying activity of Jesus Christ. At the same time, unity implies diversity. Unity is intended to respect particularity and diversity without homogenizing it into uniformity.

One of the difficulties often encountered in theological reflection on unity is that it does not deal with struggle and conflict. Rather, it sometimes seeks harmony in such a way as to deny points of oppression and injustice. The study provided redefinition of what unity looks like. It has emphasized, first of all, locating the boundaries that include and exclude, a powerful sign in the AIDS crisis; one reflected on in many of the life stories, and developed especially in chapter 4. Identifying those boundaries and naming the forces of exclusion can lead to transcending them, as Bull's early case study showed so powerfully. The Metropolitan Community Church, itself an excluded denomination, has become a source for a new sense of unity in the whole church by its leadership in responding to the AIDS crisis.

One of the aims of this study, then, has been to look for the mark of unity along the boundaries that are redrawn in situations of struggle, and to see how that redrawing of boundaries changes the experience and understanding of the church. Unity is seen less from the center than from the shifting periphery. At the same time, if God is indeed standing with PWAs and those who struggle with them, then this perspective on unity is still rooted in the unity of God. Its experience, however fleeting and provisional, is nonetheless real.

Holy Church

The traditional understanding of the church as holy is rooted in the church's close relation to God, expressed especially in the dwelling of the Holy Spirit within the church. The holiness of the church derives from the holiness of God. Marjorie Suchocki developed this idea more fully in the previous chapter.

The Unity and Renewal study's reflections on the life stories offer a number of points germane to the mark of the church as holy. In terms of the traditional understanding of the dwelling of the Holy Spirit within the church, the experience of communities of struggle would see the Holy Spirit as manifested in the prophetic activity of the church, where the Spirit provokes the church on behalf of God. A number of the life stories in chapter 10 describe churches having come alive to the challenge of AIDS. Action on the periphery prompts another understanding of holiness, a form Edward Schillebeeckx, Johannes Metz, and Dorothee Soelle have identified as "political holiness." This holiness, or union with God, is not marked by withdrawal from the world but by engagement in situations of struggle and conflict where God is especially manifest.

A second dimension of holiness grew out of a discussion of the need for constant repentance on the part of the church.[5] Such a sense of repentance is a sign of the presence of the Spirit within the church, and prompts a continuing awareness of sin and injustice and of the need to turn away from them and back to God.

These two insights into the nature of the church as holy prompted our rethinking of this mark. First, once again, the measure of the mark is how well the church acts at its periphery, not at its center. Is the church politically holy, is it acutely aware of failing the human community, and is it willing to repent of this? In so doing, the church not only shows its union with God, but helps the world see where God is most active—in the brokenness and alienation of the human community, in situations such as the AIDS crisis.

Second, the church is recognized as holy where the spirit of prophecy is alive within it. Prophecy is directed both to the church itself and to the world in which the church lives. The experience of the Unity and Renewal study would especially emphasize the latter dimension, in which the church announces justice and denounces the forces that hinder the appearance of that justice.

Catholic Church

The church as catholic has generally been understood in two ways. On one hand, its catholicity referred to its universality, the communion among all the
churches in the known world. The mark was seen,
then, in terms of the church's extension. Those who
are part of this great communion are part of the church
catholic.

The other understanding of catholic had to do with
the orthodoxy of its teaching. Those churches that held
to the orthodox faith, especially in times of persecution, could claim to be catholic, by having maintained
the faith in its entirety and in its integrity.

Our study offered perspectives on this mark of the
church as well. It has reminded us of the quality of
connectedness that is part of catholicity as extension.
Put another way, the experience of the case studies of
AIDS would prompt us to define catholicity especially
in terms of solidarity. In so doing, this question is
raised: With whom are we united, and from whom are
we separated, in situations of struggle? Bull's early
AIDS case study asked where the church ought to stand
vis-à-vis many who felt alienated from the church, yet
who sought healing in their lives in the face of fatal
disease.

In regard to the second traditional understanding of
catholicity as orthodox doctrine, the Unity and Renewal study's experience would lead to accentuating
the orthopraxis side of true doctrine. "True" here is
meant in the sense of fitting correctly or being adequate. The way in which reflection moved in the AIDS
study, from facing the horror of disease to the questions of death, resurrection, forgiveness, and acceptance, might be understood as authenticating the line
of reflection as "true" to the tradition, and therefore

orthodox. It showed more clearly the fundamental connection between reaction to a crisis and some of the
central Christian beliefs.

The Unity and Renewal study's experience, then, reminds us that to be catholic means more than being
confessionally or jurisdictionally connected; it tests the
quality of that connectedness, especially its solidarity
with those on the periphery of church and society. It
also tests catholicity to see that it is more than confession on the lips, and whether it reaches into a dynamic
relation of praxis where genuine truth can be discerned.

Apostolic Church

The church as apostolic is rooted in the idea that the
church of today is in continuity with the apostolic church
of the first century. That continuity, however, is open to
differing understandings. For some, it has meant the almost physical connection with the apostles, marked by
an unbroken chain reaching from the commissioning of
contemporary leadership back to the commissioning of
the apostles by Christ. For others, the emphasis lies more
on the quality of living, as Ignatius of Antioch put it, "in
the manner of the apostles." Such living involves orthodoxy of doctrine, missionary activity, and a realization of
the ideals of the primitive church.

The study's experience calls for a closer examination of
the meaning of continuity as the basis for apostolicity.
From the perspective of those who feel the brokenness
and alienation of human life in general and from the
church in particular, continuity can be understood as
those who do not suffer choosing to ignore the disrup-
tions of the human community. That sentiment is evident
in a number of the stories in this book, where employers,
family, and churches find the presence of a PWA as disruptive and dangerous. For the church to be truly apostolic, it must seek continuity not only in an embracing of

those things it considers potentially disruptive, but also in constancy in advocacy for justice. By always being at the point of discontinuity—that is, of being with those who are excluded or ignored—can the church hope to maintain fidelity to the cross and to Christ. This seems to be the principal contribution of the Unity and Renewal study to the understanding of apostolicity.

PROPHETIC CHURCH?

Should a fifth mark of the church be added, that of the church as prophetic? The study group was not of one mind on this.

On the one hand, making prophecy the fifth mark would highlight a constitutive element of being church, much as does unity, holiness, catholicity, and apostolicity. On the other hand, prophecy has already been discussed, especially in light of holiness. And, perhaps more important, the prophetic character of the church may not be a specific characteristic of the church as much as it is the lens through which *all* aspects of the church are to be seen. Moreover, to separate prophecy from the other four allows the other four to continue to be understood in the traditional way. A fifth mark of prophecy "takes care" of the prophetic dimension and can leave the other dimensions untouched by the insights from the case studies that were considered.

However this latter point is resolved, it still stands that the approach followed in the Unity and Renewal study can offer considerable insight into ecumenical ecclesiology, not only in furthering the frontiers of our knowledge and common quest for unity, but also by helping us rethink traditional categories of theology in new and challenging ways.

9   *Letty M. Russell*

A Church for Troubled Waters

New opportunities for self-understanding often come in the midst of troubled waters, and in such situations we can sometimes discover God's Spirit at work. In fact, the troubling of the waters is a metaphor not only for times of difficulty but also for the presence of God's Spirit.[1] In Genesis 1:1, it is the Spirit that is soaring over the uncreated, watery chaos as God begins to create the heavens and the earth. In Matthew 3:11–17, the symbol of new life is the water of deliverance used in baptism. In John 5:1–18, the man by the pool of Bethesda is waiting for the Spirit to trouble the waters so that he can be the first to enter the pool and be healed.

John's story about the man waiting for God's healing power is a good example of this ambiguous metaphor of "troubling," for in the story the troubling refers to divine action, but also foreshadows the trouble and suffering that comes to those who identify with "outsiders." There is no indication of why Jesus picks this man to heal, except that this man has no friends and he needs help. Many of the parallel healing stories in the other Gospels, like the one in Mark 2, include friends who help the man reach Jesus, but here in John's story the man, paralyzed for thirty-eight years, has "no [one] to put [him] into the pool when the water is troubled" (John 5:7).

From the point of view of those suffering with AIDS, there is no question that this is a major issue raised by the text. Why aren't there more friends? Why doesn't the government, the community, the United Nations, the *church* act as friend to those who are waiting for drugs, protection, and care, yet who often end up dying alone on the street outside their village, or in the hospital, denied their human dignity? In the United States, neither the government nor the churches have been willing to go all out in taking the side of the victim.[2] Instead, there has been widespread collusion in blaming the victim and in viewing the spread of AIDS as a punishment for a homosexual lifestyle. Thus, in *AIDS Issues: Confronting the Challenge,* David Hallman writes:

> In the near absence of constructive leadership by churches on these issues, the public has been left with the judgmental theological attitudes voiced by some conservative church spokespersons and TV evangelists that AIDS is God's punishment of homosexuals and IV drug users.[3]

The refusal of churches to befriend those suffering with AIDS is all the more striking when we consider that it is Jesus himself who befriends those who are the outcasts of religion and society, seeking to heal those who are sick and welcoming those who are outsiders into God's realm. In the case of the man by the pool of Bethesda, Jesus becomes his friend, enabling him to take up his pallet and walk even without the healing waters. As John 5 tells the story, this healing on the Sabbath is not without cost. Jesus is challenged by the Temple authorities for breaking the law of no work on the Sabbath. His reply serves only to antagonize them, for he says that, like God, he must be constantly at work in order to bring healing and justice to the creation.

In the story, it is Jesus himself who becomes the troubler of the waters. Perhaps it is the pain involved in Jesus' way, identification with the outcast, that often leads churches to ignore the reality of AIDS and to neglect their ministry of healing and justice. Yet the testimony of this book is that the struggle with AIDS is one of the ways the Spirit is speaking to the church. The "troublemakers" seem to have become the prophets who call out to the church to reexamine its traditional self-understanding and to look at its accustomed forms of ministry.

ECCLESIOLOGY AND THE IMAGINATION OF AIDS

A traditional way of describing what it means to be the church is to talk about the marks or signs of the church. As Robert Schreiter has pointed out, these defining characteristics of the church that are clearly evident for all to see are usually drawn from the addition made "to the Nicene Creed by the Council of Constantinople in 381: '[and in] one holy catholic and apostolic church' " [ch. 8, p. 122]. Discussion begins here with a creed recognized by Orthodox, Roman Catholic, and Protestant traditions, but one which moves to other signs as well, and becomes controversial as one confessional body begins to consider the marks of another invalid. Thus, at the time of the Reformation, the discussion of whether the Protestant or the Roman Catholic church had the true marks and was truly church was very much part of the persecution and religious wars of the sixteenth and seventeenth centuries in Europe. Unity among churches, based on mutual recognition of one another as communities of faith in Jesus Christ, still involves us in the question of the identity of the church of Christ.

Why is it important to ask when a church of Jesus

Christ is a church? In times of change we seek to understand who we are in a new situation. The crises of our times, including the crisis of AIDS, confront the church with the need to understand what it means to be the body of Christ, sharing in suffering and in the ministry of Christ in today's world. As we begin to explore our self-understanding, we find that such descriptions are helpful for locating ourselves within the Christian tradition and discerning indicators of faithfulness, even though they are clearly *not* helpful as rules used to exclude others. They are part of our search for ecclesial clues that point beyond themselves to God's intention for the new creation.

It is possible that what Mary Catherine Bateson and Richard Goldsby call the imagination of AIDS may become the imagination not only of human unity and the interdependent web of life but also of church unity in the name of the one who is Friend.[4] The cooperative support and new imagination it takes to work against this worldwide epidemic may indeed teach us about new ways of living with one another. Sharing in this struggle may very well lead us to a new understanding of the identity of the church: the church with AIDS.

Rethinking a Reformed Understanding of the Church

In the Reformation of the sixteenth century and beyond, there was a long period of controversial theology in which the Protestant Reformers and their descendants argued against the Roman Catholic reformers and their descendants about what made the church truly church. The Protestants claimed that the true church was not only recognized by the visible signs (*signa*) of oneness, holiness, catholicity, and apostolicity, but also by what they called the marks (*nota*) or distinguishing characteristics of the church. These marks were claimed to be what obviously constituted the church as the true church, namely, "where the word is truly preached and the sacraments rightly administered." They did not deny the importance of the Nicene formula, but they wanted to build their reformation on the scriptures. For this reason they tried to discern in the biblical tradition how the church might be faithful in its preaching and sacramental life. Today it is generally recognized by Roman Catholics that the witness of the scriptures to Jesus Christ is the basis of the life of the church.[5] It is also recognized generally by Protestants that, as Jürgen Moltmann says,

> A church in which the gospel is purely preached and the sacraments are rightly used is the one, holy, catholic and apostolic church. The two Reformation signs of the church really only show from within what the traditional attributes of the church describe from without, so to speak.[6]

The word purely or truly preached was understood by the Reformers to be preaching according to the scriptures. They took great pains to educate the people in the reading and study of the Bible so that they could know what was "true." For instance, John Calvin wrote his *Institutes of the Christian Religion* in order to guide the interpretation of scriptures, so that students of theology could be prepared for "the reading of the divine word."[7] Then as now, true interpretation of the Bible was a difficult task. In every time and place, we have to seek out again what the true Gospel message is for our time. But at least it can be said that the Gospels witness to the story of a man who proclaimed God's reign and welcomed people, all people, as children of God. Jesus proclaimed the good news that the outsiders, those rejected by the society and the religious establishment, were nevertheless made welcome by God.

Whatever else the true preaching of the word would need to include, it at least would have to be a word that speaks from the perspective of those who have been crushed and marginalized in our society. It would need to be a word of solidarity, healing, and love in situations of brokenness and despair. This word would often be disturbing and troubling to those who have hopes of "making it." But it is clearly an important word from the one whom we call Friend. An example of this type of true preaching comes to us from the witness of the Metropolitan Community Church. This denomination applied for admission to the National Council of Churches in 1981. As Beryl Ingram-Ward points out in chapter 4, the church met all the requirements of membership, but the NCC governing board decided not to act on its application because the church openly and affirmingly welcomed homosexual persons as members [ch. 4, p. 75]. Nevertheless, it has often been the MCC churches that have reached out to persons with AIDS, and to other churches in ecumenical coalitions of caring. The scriptures have very little to say about homosexuality, but they have a great deal to say on the necessity of hospitality and of reaching out to those who are oppressed (Luke 4:18–19).[8]

In the light of ministry with persons with AIDS, it is important to stress that in our time we are learning that the word purely or truly preached is a word that must be heard as good news by those who are marginalized and oppressed. This discovery is one of the gifts of the Spirit that has been emphasized by many liberation theologians, for, as we listen to the scriptures as good news to the poor and suffering, and as we listen to the poor explaining the meaning of Jesus' welcome to us, we may more truly understand the gospel message of God's love [ch. 12, p. 175].

The sacraments rightly administered were also understood by the Reformers to mean sacraments instituted and administered according to the teaching of the scriptures. Protesting against the abuses of the sacraments in the sixteenth-century church, they emphasized baptism and the Lord's Supper as the two sacraments instituted by Christ's words and actions. They made sure that preparation for the sacraments included instruction in their biblical meaning, and they practiced "fencing of the table," by allowing only members in good standing to receive the elements of bread and wine. There also continues to be much discussion over the meaning of baptism and the Eucharist, although there is much that churches can say together about these institutions and their meaning. For instance, the *Baptism, Eucharist and Ministry* document of Faith and Order says that Christian baptism is rooted in the ministry, death, and resurrection of Jesus of Nazareth (Matt. 28:18–20). "It is incorporation into Christ, who is the crucified and risen Lord; it is entry into the New Covenant between God and God's people."[9] Eucharist is interpreted through the words of 1 Corinthians 11:23–25 and is "a sacramental meal which by visible signs communicates to us God's love in Jesus Christ."[10]

When we seek to understand what it would mean to administer the sacraments *rightly,* we need to give consideration to what the biblical meaning of "rightly" would be. Certainly that meaning would go beyond proper preparation, administration, and celebration of the words and actions of Jesus. In fact, the word "rightly" probably would include the need for the community of celebration to live out a life of righteousness or justice. Such an idea is clearly conveyed by Matthew 25:31–46. This parable of the "last judgment" seems to reflect Jesus' own history of identification with the poor and the outcast so that, together with the Messiah, all who hunger and thirst, all who are naked, sick, or in prison, become the real presence of God's mending work. In the feeding and caring for the least of our brothers and sisters, we discover that Christ is present with them to teach us about righteousness and justice.

The biblical meaning of righteousness is justice, or "putting things right." Those who share with God in mending the creation share in God's justice. The sacraments are about God reaching out on the cross to make things right, and about God's continuing action on behalf of groaning creation. Here we find the gift of righteousness and justice, and are called to right administration of those gifts together with others in need of God's justice. Thus the "fencing of the table" at the Lord's Supper still refers to the need to be properly prepared to receive God's gifts of love and grace, but it does not mean that those who are marginal to church or society should be disinvited (Luke 14:15–24).

The fenced table becomes what in the black church tradition is called the welcome table.[11] This welcome table is the communion table and every other church table gathering that symbolizes the fact that those who have been denied access to the table of the white, rich masters are welcomed at God's table, and are offered a foretaste of that final moment of full partnership with God.[12] In one of her early stories titled "The Welcome Table," Alice Walker tells of this powerful message of God's welcome by sharing the story of an old black woman who, on being thrown out of the white church where she had tried to rest and pray, met up with Jesus on the hot dusty road, and walked and talked with him. How long she talked no one knows, but it was at least long enough to find her way home to God's table. They found her body alongside the road the next day.[13]

The sacraments are the foretaste of God's future. The table rightly prepared is a table that belongs to God, where all things are held in common. Having prepared for the table, we discern Christ's body not only in the broken bread but also in the broken people of the world. And if we welcome them, we may receive the gift of a renewed church; a church that makes outsiders welcome, as they sing, "We're gonna sit at the welcome table one of these days!" In the black church tradition, "Welcome Table" is sung as a sign that all are welcome to eat at God's banquet table. It is no accident that this is the table that is spread at MCC churches and other churches carrying out an extensive AIDS ministry. Everyone is welcome, and even those who have to be carried by others are greeted and encircled with love at a table rightly administered in the name of God's justice and love [ch. 4, p. 77].

When we look at the Reformers' "marks" of the church in the light of AIDS, we notice that the marks themselves involve us in actions of justice and love that prepare the table. It would seem that we need this emphasis in the interpretation of the marks, or that we need to add an additional mark that reminds us that the identity of the church, grounded in scripture, is the identity of its Lord who has identified himself with the least of his brothers and sisters and is willing to pay the cost of working for their inclusion. In the light of the imagination of AIDS, it seems that the word truly preached and sacraments rightly administered are found in communities of faith and struggle. For the church's identity is derived from the story of Jesus' own word and action on the cross, in solidarity with the oppressed. This is our word and action as well, as we struggle for justice and life itself together with our sisters and brothers with AIDS.

Rethinking a Creedal Understanding of the Church

In chapter 8, Robert Schreiter describes the many ways that the creedal understanding of the church shifts when we interpret "one holy catholic and apostolic" from the point of view of those at the periphery of life, society, and the church. As with the other identifying marks, what is of most importance is not the presence of certain characteristics, but their use and practice. According to Hans Küng,

> Unity, holiness, catholicity and apostolicity are therefore not only gifts, granted to the Church by God's grace, but at the same time tasks which it is vital for the Church to fulfil in a responsible way.[14]

Unity includes action for justice. Holiness includes the experience of shared suffering; "the common experience of suffering and the common action to alleviate it."[15] Catholicity includes connection to the world as well as orthopraxy in service. Apostolicity includes "constancy in advocacy for justice" [ch. 8, p. 132].

Many other contemporary theologians assert that these dimensions of the church need to include the perspective of people on the periphery or margins and they very much need an emphasis on the dimension of prophecy or justice. For instance, a special consultation, held in 1984, on one common expression of the apostolic faith from the perspective of black Christians in the United States placed heavy emphasis on this dimension. In this report, "Toward a Common Expression of Faith: A Black North American Perspective," they affirm "that the One, Holy church cannot exist apart from ministries of justice and liberation."[16]

In chapters 7 and 8, both Suchocki and Schreiter expand the mark of holiness to make this emphasis clear. Schreiter specifically argues that the reinterpretation is better done within the four creedal marks so that the prophetic dimension is seen throughout [ch. 8, p. 132]. But just as the word truly preached and the sacraments rightly administered need the dimension of the community of struggle for justice, it would seem that there does need to be a fifth mark of justice. A shift in perspective to those who are oppressed is crucial, and it seems to me that this perspective is very difficult to maintain without a fifth mark, that of justice.

The sinfulness of the church is such that a constant and equal reminder of its nature as a community of justice is crucial for its identity. This reminder needs to push all churches to constant self-critique and expansion of their understanding of justice. For example, black churches have historically been steadfast in their advocacy of racial and economic justice, but have often ignored the issues of justice for women and for homosexual persons.[17] The latter issue has contributed to the reluctance of many black churches to be involved in programs addressing needs of persons with AIDS. This picture is beginning to change, especially with increasing numbers of I.V. drug users and women and children of color who are HIV positive. More and more black churches are following in the path of the First Iconium Baptist Church in making new justice connections [ch. 12, p. 175].

The same need for continuing self-critique in the light of the mark of justice is needed in white feminist theology and in Women-Church. Women-Church is an exodus movement of women seeking out communities that express their full humanity and liberation from patriarchy. Small feminist base communities gathered for shared worship seek to live out the mark of justice for all women. Often, however, they neglect the issues of justice for persons of all color and class, because they are largely white and middle-class. In a similar way,

the MCC San Francisco congregation has had to struggle to include men of color, and women of all colors, in
their programs [ch. 11, p. 171].

The dualism between church and world that is criti-
cized by Suchocki, as well as by Arthur Freeman in
chapter 5, is so much a way of thought and life of
the contemporary, white middle-class church in the
United States that it is very difficult to learn to be a
community of struggle, a community of love and justice. For this to happen, the churches will need to repent of their double sin. Most of our churches cannot
respond to the need for justice and liberation as a fundamental part of their calling as the church of Jesus
Christ because they have reversed the teaching of
Paul, that we need to be in, but not of, the world.

According to Robin Scroggs, Paul reminds the Corinthians that they are to continue to participate in the life
of their communities, but they are to live as if the new
creation were already at hand (1 Cor. 7:31).[18] Instead,
the churches of our day often live of, but not in, the
world. Their lives, structures, class divisions, sexual orientation, and prejudices all reflect the culture of which
they are a part rather than the new creation. All the
while, they refuse to be involved in social, economic,
and political advocacy for justice. Only true repentance and willingness to be in, but not of, the world will
lead members of the churches to search for their identity in the midst of troubled waters.

FOLLOWING THE TROUBLEMAKER

This investigation of a church for troubled waters
began with the story of the man by the pool of Bethesda who was healed on the Sabbath. Jesus himself became the troubler of the waters when he broke the
Sabbath law by healing the man. His conflict with the

religious authorities over God's concern for the outcast put him in the position of being considered a trouble-maker. The mark of his work for justice was that of a cross and nails in his hands and feet.[19]

Through this healing story, we learn that the church needs to be willing to stir up the water, rather than look for the closest "bridge over troubled waters." If it is water that has been stirred up by God's Spirit, it may still hold a great deal of risk for those who swim in it, but it will be a place where we are likely to find strength for the journey. And if it is water that is stirred up by injustice and the marginalization of those considered "other," then the church also needs to be present there to work for change.

The search for identity in the church and the discussion of descriptive marks has caused a great deal of suffering and mutual condemnation over the centuries. Yet that search could also become the basis for living as a church with AIDS. A church for troubled waters follows a Lord who is working still to call us all to take part in the work of mending the creation and putting it right (John 5:17). What we have learned through reflection on shared ministry with persons with AIDS is that love with justice is at the heart of what the church is about. For the church continues to be a community baptized in the troubled waters of the Spirit and called out by God to participate in the new creation.

PART FOUR

The Church with AIDS

Having moved around the theological spiral of engagement from experience to response and analysis and to new questioning of the tradition, we now come to alternative suggestions for study and action. In some books, this section would be a separate study guide, or in an appendix, but here it is made the fourth part of the book as a reminder that theology is shaped by action and leads to action. Our study of the church with AIDS includes ways that our understanding of the church and the crisis of AIDS shifts as we begin to work for justice and healing together with others.

Chapter 10 contains nine stories of persons and churches living with AIDS. The stories, edited by Shannon Clarkson, were included for two reasons: first, to share some of these stories gathered by the working group as a basis for our reflections; second, for use in study and discussion groups. Many pastors, teachers, laypersons, and students may want to make use of this section as an entry point for discussion of the implications of living with AIDS in their local situation.

To assist in further discovering the implications of AIDS for action in the churches, the last three chapters lift up the role of the church in the struggle with AIDS. In chapter 11, "We Are the Church Alive," Kittredge

Cherry and James Mitulski describe the ministry of MCC San Francisco among the gay community and among those who have AIDS in San Francisco. This chapter can be used with chapters 1, 2, and 4, as it provides a contextual description of the church where Ron Russell-Coons is sharing in ministry, and where Beryl Ingram-Ward found herself profoundly welcomed at the welcome table.

In chapter 12, Katharine Sakenfeld invites us all to do a new reading of the good Samaritan parable and to ask again, Who is my neighbor? In a sense, her chapter is a response to all the other chapters, and puts together the pieces of the story with contemporary experience and asks for our response. As we look to our denominations for guidance in the struggle against AIDS, we can find a sample of denominational responses in the three reports in chapter 13, "Resources for Study and Action." Addresses for denominational information are also included in the selected bibliography. In addition, Shannon Clarkson, working with members of the writing group, has collected some sample worship resources and provided a set of questions that can be used as a guide for study and discussion of the chapters.

This book has many different elements, but they all belong together as part of the theological spiral. Study of the church with AIDS provides many clues to renewal in the midst of crisis, but those clues will have no meaning if churches in the United States and around the world do not confess that, indeed, "We are the church with AIDS," and that we have been called to renewal by taking up the task of healing and justice.

10 *J. Shannon Clarkson, editor*

Life Stories

DAVID'S STORY

Living with AIDS has forced a complete transformation in my values and priorities. Faced with the threat of death, I have become aware of the value of life, the value of each day. I have also discovered the importance of the inner, spiritual life. People with AIDS are increasingly turning to non-medical resources to support their health, and many are learning to cultivate their spiritual lives. I have incorporated meditation and prayer into my daily living and feel I have not only benefited spiritually, but physically as well. In addition, a real healing has occurred between my parents and me. I'm just sorry it took something like AIDS to bring us together.

It has been almost three years since I began experiencing the first symptoms of AIDS. In these three years, my life has changed in ways I could not have imagined. It has not been an easy journey. At one point I went through a period of deep depression, and was close to suicide. I have experienced times when I felt isolated and alone. I have experienced the meaning of hopelessness. But as I have worked to transform my life, I have discovered that hope is the key to survival, and I no longer permit myself to believe that a diagnosis of AIDS is an automatic death sentence. Despite the statistics, despite the friends I have lost, I expect the best

149

from each day, and I expect my life to continue to have value and meaning for as long as I am alive.

David had been an English language teacher in Japan only seven months when he was diagnosed as HIV positive. Following David's earlier revelation to his parents that he was gay, his relationship with his parents had been rather strained. In Japan he was sharing an apartment with his friend Robert.

The realization that something was seriously wrong with his body came slowly to David. Neither the Japanese doctors he consulted nor David himself imagined that the physical difficulties he was experiencing might be related to AIDS. Not until his condition was so serious that he could no longer function and had to be hospitalized was the diagnosis made. Had he been in the United States, his condition undoubtedly would have been diagnosed earlier.

Although David tried to continue teaching in Japan, when no hospital in Japan would admit him it became obvious that he should return to the United States for treatment. His roommate arranged for his airline tickets and sent David off to Seattle, his former home, as well as arranging for his medical care there. Three weeks later, David was able to leave the hospital but was no longer able to work.

Ron Russell-Coons

CAROLE'S STORY

Carole is a writer and an activist living in San Francisco. Some years ago, Carole received numerous transfusions taken from the San Francisco Blood Bank. At the prompting of friends and associates, Carole finally had her blood tested. Her journals speak of the "roller coaster" feelings she has had since finding out that she is HIV positive.

Women with the AIDS virus often find that although many support services exist for gay males who are HIV positive, this is not the case for women. Carole goes to a church that has an active AIDS ministry. Its HIV-positive support group draws from twenty to thirty people each month. Carole is the only woman. She does, however, have four or five women in her life who are able to provide nurture, even though they do not have AIDS.

At this point, Carole has not had any major opportunistic infections. She receives treatment at San Francisco General Hospital since she does not have insurance. Lately, neuropathy has developed, so she occasionally wears a leg brace. Her journals talk about fevers and other HIV-related symptoms.

Anonymity is still an issue for Carole. A strong advocate and activist for human rights since the sixties, she still has deep concern over the negative reactions that are possible. What will others think of me? How reliable are my friends? Carole is searching for answers.

Recently Carole attended a family reunion in Montana. Her doctor in San Francisco urged her to tell her family about her HIV infection. Like so many others, Carole imagined the scene over and over before it actually happened. Life in Montana can be far removed from the reality of a "big city disease" like AIDS. After all, the vast majority of Americans still believe that only gay men have AIDS. As Carole opened up to her family and became vulnerable, she discovered that they were educated about AIDS and were more than willing to be comforting and supportive.

Carole has worked through telling a few friends and her immediate family. Business is in order. Now she can get on with living.

Ron Russell-Coons

HECTOR'S STORY: AIDS AND THE CHURCH IN PUERTO RICO

Hector was born and raised in Puerto Rico. By age ten, he became aware of his homosexual feelings and, despite the social taboos against it, regularly engaged in sexual experimentation with several of his male cousins and friends. When he began getting into trouble at thirteen he left home.

L'Anni Hill-Alto

I was born to a poor family in a small town. Before I was two years old, my father, who had been physically abusive to my mother, deserted the family. My mother and grandmother raised me and my five brothers and sisters. We regularly attended the Roman Catholic Church in the town, but I never had any particular feelings for the church; they didn't pay much attention to me. By age ten I no longer attended church.

At age twenty, I decided to go to New York City. For two months I slept in the streets, on tenement rooftops and trains, unable to find a job because I didn't speak English. Finally, someone took me to St. Mark's, a church shelter for homeless youth, where I found some security. They found me a job as a dishwasher and gave me a counselor to talk to. I bounced from job to job, shelter to shelter, and finally moved in with a man, but that didn't work out. I developed a rectal abscess and needed an operation, but the Lincoln Hospital on 169th Street denied it to me, because I had no money; I couldn't work with the abscess as bad as it was. I lived in shelters for about a year. They allowed me to work in the shelter as a receptionist with the Department of Social Services, in their "breakthrough program." This was one of the best jobs I had.

A nurse in the shelter arranged for me to have the operation, but as soon as I returned to the shelter, I got very sick. I eventually went back to Puerto Rico, where I learned I had AIDS. When I told my family, they immediately kicked me out of the house. I felt like a leper. I began attending a small evangelical church. When I spoke with the pastor he insisted that I repent of my homosexuality and forbade the bus driver to bring me to the church.

In May, 1988, I was asked to appear on a local television program which had dedicated a week of its programming to AIDS. I explained how I'd been repeatedly neglected by the hospitals. The Secretary of Health saw it, and challenged the hospital policies regarding treatment of AIDS patients. That afternoon, an ambulance came by and took me to the hospital. However, I waited there from 3 P.M. till 1 the following morning before a doctor saw me. He discharged me immediately. I had no way to get home, so I asked the police for a ride to the town boundary, then walked home. I decided I had to get more help, so the next day I called the AIDS Foundation, and since then I've received the support necessary to maintain myself. I've tried to abstain from sex, but . . . I've got my needs. I took a lover for two months recently, but he's an addict, and got arrested. He's in jail now.

Since last September, I've been gaining weight, and feeling good about myself. Now I know God loves me because I'm getting better. I feel much closer to him. I feel like I'm really a child of God. He's the only one who can take my life away. How can the church help me? I don't trust the church—they fight too much. Actually, I wonder if God isn't making me better because he wants *me* to start a church.

OUR BABIES

Two African-American infant girls, born only months apart, were placed in a foster care home together. Both were born addicted to cocaine and both were determined to be in the "extremely high risk" category for developing AIDS.

When we were first asked to be foster parents to AIDS babies, neither of us, being single, career-minded women, had children of her own. We were a little awed by the responsibil-

ity for the care of infants and more than a little nervous about
the changes in lifestyle this would create. But, more than this,
we were determined that no baby should have to remain in a
hospital because there was no one to take her home. We are
both religious people and have always looked to God to guide
us and help us in making decisions. It was no time at all before God convicted our hearts that we were to do all we could
to provide a loving and happy home to whatever children
were given into our care.

Because of the misconceptions about children and AIDS,
we have chosen to tell very few people about our babies'
medical condition. However, we have been blessed by those
persons who do know who have stood by us, and supported
and encouraged us. As well as learning firsthand how truly
cruel people can be, we have also learned how absolutely
wonderful other people can be.

Caring for our babies, like caring for any infants, is a difficult undertaking. Because the development of a healthy immune system is critical to an HIV-positive infant, we
followed strict guidelines to protect them from unnecessary
exposure to dangerous germs. We sanitized everything they
touched. All of their clothes were bleached and double
rinsed after each wearing. Much of our house and most of its
contents were sanitized with bleach at least weekly; the task
was endless. Fortunately, our care seems to be helping.
The babies are now beginning to test "non-reactive" with
the HIV blood tests, which means they have moved from
the high risk category to the "probably won't contract"
category.

Have they licked it? We pray so, but that is only one part
of their battle. They have been so brave and so loving all
through this struggle and now are at a time when they are
beginning to make their own lives. They play with the
neighbor children and are naturally beginning to stretch
their boundaries. Will they someday meet you? Will you be
their school bus driver? their teacher? their neighbor? Most
important, will you be their friend, or, after all of their struggle, will they only now learn who the real enemy is?

J. Tamshel

No Name

The streets of San Francisco, like the streets of many other big cities, are a home for the homeless. A handsome, blond, blue-eyed young man waits daily at the corner of Market and Castro streets, and asks for quarters. The keen observer will spot the signs of thrush, a yeast infection, as the man asks for spare change. His arms reveal bluish-purple spots: Kaposi's sarcoma.

Whatever caused this man to become a street person is not important. What is shocking is that this man—this very sick man—lives on the street, without the kind of medical attention that he needs; that he deserves as a human being. I wonder how many people pass him every day and judge him. Perhaps they don't even notice. His story is titled "No Name," because for me, and for the countless others who pass him each day, he has no name. And, as "No Name," he represents the thousands of homeless persons who, for so many of us, have no name.

Writes the Rev. Donald Jackson, superintendent of a San Francisco rescue mission,

> Depending on whose estimate you believe, there are between 2,500 and 4,000 homeless homosexuals in San Francisco. About a third of the gay homeless are homeless for the same reasons that straights are homeless—substance abuse, mental disorders, retardation, lack of job skills, just plain bad luck. There are between 350 and 650 homeless people with AIDS and at least as many more with ARC (AIDS-related conditions) who are too sick—mentally and physically—to work or cope with the welfare bureaucracy.[1]

I really wonder about him. How long will he be able to survive? Maybe he doesn't want to survive. What's my responsibility? I could send him to one of the AIDS charities. But what can they provide for a homeless person? Again, Rev. Jackson:

> Someone who lives in a doorway has no use for a bag of groceries. All charities and religious organizations help the hungry, take in the fatigued, give coats and blankets to the cold, send the sick to the doctor, but they do nothing to solve the underlying problems of the homeless.[2]

Ron Russell-Coons

JANE'S STORY: THE SCARLET A

I wear the Scarlet A. I keep it well hidden. You may never see me cry or realize from my appearance that I have been infected by the virus. Nevertheless, I have been shattered. I need love, compassion, and community to help me make it from day to day. I have done nothing immoral or illegal to contract this disease, but those who have hurt just as deeply as I. Their needs are as great or greater than mine for a compassionate and loving response to AIDS.[3]

Jane was infected with the AIDS virus by a blood transfusion when pregnant with her first child. As a result, the child also contracted AIDS. Having no idea that she was carrying the AIDS virus, two years after the birth of her first child Jane became pregnant again. When the new baby was five months old, she received a call from the blood bank saying the donor who had given blood for her transfusion had AIDS.

The second child was born prematurely with multiple medical problems. Within two months, Jane's world fell apart. The baby was in critical condition with only weeks or days to live. Her husband lost his job and career when his employer found out that his family had been touched by AIDS. Her older child had to be removed from her day-care program. They were asked not to return to their church. They fled to another city, too terrified to risk further harassment and persecution.

In a few months, the baby died. To protect herself and her family, Jane formed only superficial relationships to avoid questions. She couldn't share the fact that every time she looked at her two-year-old little girl her heart was breaking. She couldn't share the fact that her marriage was fragmenting from the intolerable stress. She couldn't share her "sickness," lest someone get suspicious. And certainly she couldn't share the severity of her daughter's illness, for fear that the child would be totally ostracized.

Jane was in a new city with no friends, no church, no home, no job, a struggling marriage, a very sick child, and ever-present grief for her baby who had died. She reached out to a local Baptist church. The pastor was supportive, but when he asked parents in the congregation about the possibility of the child's attending Sunday school, the parents said "No." Jane does not attend church now.

R. Page Fulgham

CARL'S STORY: MOVED TO ACT

Plymouth Congregational United Church of Christ in Des Moines, a parish of three thousand members, became involved in an educational program about homosexuality and AIDS when a prominent lay leader of the congregation developed AIDS. The senior pastor responded to the news of Carl's illness in three ways. First, he educated himself on the issues. Second, he organized a month-long educational program for eleven other area clergy. Third, he talked with Carl about the best ways to prepare the congregation.

Even while hospitalized, Carl, a high officer in state

government, was nominated to become chair of a major church board. To my knowledge, none of the other board members knew that he was gay, let alone infected with AIDS. I pledged my support and he agreed to accept election.

He also agreed that I could share his story with a dozen selected church leaders before I left for vacation. Neither of us knew when he might become incapacitated, but both of us knew that, if and when he had to resign his state position, it would be a major news story.

My meetings with those lay leaders were among the most moving of my entire ministry. Though the leaders vary in theological perspective and in their attitudes toward homosexuality, their response, in every case, was compassion; compassionate support for Carl. And, I felt, a new readiness to reexamine old assumptions.

Essentially, I told them Carl's whole story, and answered any questions candidly; I shared with them printed materials about homosexuality and AIDS to take home and read; I told them the stand I was going to take on the issues and that I hoped, as lay leaders of the church, they would be able to stand with me.

Carl told me later of the several who contacted him to express their concern and support. As this is being written, Carl is in excellent health, giving vigorous leadership. And all of us who know pray for the miracle.

As a result of the clergy cluster gatherings, a five-session educational program entitled "Compassion: A Response to AIDS" was offered to the Des Moines community and hosted by the Plymouth church. The sessions included medical information as well as discussions of homophobia and issues related to homosexuality. "Religious Implications" was the final topic, presented by two area pastors. A Lutheran male pastor with a Ph.D. in theology examined scriptural references to homosexuality and offered possible interpretations to those texts. A female UCC pastor presented a theology of relationships that calls for inclusiveness, compassion, and a healing ministry on the part of the religious community toward the gay community and those with AIDS: "We are the body of Christ. If part of us has AIDS, we all have AIDS." A Plymouth man commented, "As a gay man, I feel proud that our church is courageous enough to tackle controversial social issues and to make *all* of us feel like a valued part of the family of God."

James O. Gilliom and Faith V. Ferre

CHUCK'S STORY: THE FIRST ICONIUM BAPTIST CHURCH

The First Iconium Baptist Church, located in the West End section of Atlanta, near the Atlanta University Center, is a relatively young congregation of five years with approximately three hundred fifty members. The median age of members of the congregation is thirty-seven. The African-Americans who constitute its membership include professionals and blue-collar workers who love the Lord.

The pastor of First Iconium received a call in May, 1988, from a member whose relative, Chuck, another member, was very ill. Chuck was active in the church, serving on the usher board, the community outreach committee, and the men's fellowship and often leading worship services. Chuck wanted to talk with the pastor, but was embarrassed. The pastor realized his role was crucial in determining how the congregation would react to the news of Chuck's illness, and had attended several seminars on AIDS in the black community. After talking and praying with Chuck, the pastor began the task of informing the church.

In Bible studies, sermons, Sunday school, fellowship

breakfasts, and other settings, the pastor began to mention AIDS. He offered educational materials on Sunday mornings. He then met with the committees on which Chuck served, and talked about Chuck's illness. The response of the congregation was very supportive. As the pastor says,

> We have always been a caring congregation, but working with Chuck changed drastically the way our people view sin and sinners. No longer were the derogatory, negative connotations of sin appropriate for Chuck. He was a person we all knew and loved. Chuck enabled us to realize that we all can make mistakes and it really produced a serious decline in judgmental attitudes. The relationship between Chuck and the church was so strong that when his mother and father came to take Chuck back home, he informed them that he was home at First Iconium and he wanted to spend his last days with his church family.

In the days and months that followed, the members continued to minister to Chuck and then began an outreach program to other persons with AIDS as well, particularly with children. Additional educational seminars have been held in the church and much educational material distributed to members. Says the pastor of their experience:

> The church is increasingly becoming the body of Christ, "binding up the broken-hearted and healing the sick." A truly introspective approach to the ministry has developed due to our ministering with, to, and for Chuck. The church has become the broken, tortured, bruised body of Christ restoring the world unto himself. Within the context of working with the AIDS victims, we experience firsthand our vulnerability and our inevitable destiny with death.
>
> Timothy McDonald

THE HIDDEN GRIEVERS: AIDS-Related Bereavement

The Hidden Grievers is an AIDS-related bereavement program conducted by St. Vincent's Hospital and Medical Center Supportive Care Program in New York. St. Vincent's Hospital, located in the Greenwich Village neighborhood of New York City, where there is a very large homosexual population, treats the largest number of AIDS patients in the world.

The bereavement process of partners, families, and friends who have suffered a loss from AIDS is characterized by its own particular difficulties and needs. Society has applied a traumatic stigma to the victims of this devastating disease. Their friends and families are often also identified with the disease, thus inheriting the pain of this social stigma. The result is that the ordinary channels of expressing grief are often denied to these "survivors" of AIDS; the tragic recourse is that they become the "hidden grievers." They struggle to mourn, survive, and resume their lives in an emotional catacomb. This situation demands a response from the churches. It offers another opportunity to express solidarity with the suffering.

Typically, the Hidden Grievers bereavement program at St. Vincent's consists of seven or eight participants and two coleaders. The group meets for ninety minutes once a week for eight weeks. While the majority of the participants are of homosexual orientation, there recently has been an increase in women who have lost sons or husbands. The primary purpose of the program is to assist individuals in dealing with their grief with support, comfort, counseling, and education.

The personal agony experienced by these hidden grievers underscores the numerous dimensions and consequences of the AIDS epidemic. The social stigma, the youth of the victims, and the denial of the usual sources of bereavement support characterize the uniqueness of loss because of AIDS. Often the real cause of death is explained to others under the camouflage of another diagnosis.

Many people, during periods of bereavement, think about God, their own spirituality, their church, and so on. AIDS-related bereavement brings up similar issues. However, the issues of God and the churches in this context harbor their own particularity. If alienation from the church due to lifestyles was experienced, it is not anticipated that overtures offering assistance from the churches always will be welcomed. For many homosexuals, the churches only represent a symbol of the alienation experienced in society at large. However, the support and interaction offered by the churches can be an opportunity for a positive spiritual experience in this time of crisis.

Patrick Cogan, SA

Kittredge Cherry
11   *and James Mitulski*

We Are the Church
Alive

"Heaven has as much to do with life before death as with life after death."

Steven Clover was able to voice that vision in the last months before he died of AIDS, while his body was wasting away with the effort of fighting off rare forms of cancer, pneumonia, and other diseases. Once dapper and golden-haired, he was the essence of a refined gentleman, the sort who might own a couple of jewelry stores in Boston—which he did. He also served as an assistant pastor of a black church, Union Baptist Church in Cambridge. He left all that behind in August, 1986, to attend the Pacific School of Religion in Berkeley and the Metropolitan Community Church of San Francisco (MCC San Francisco), a predominantly white church in a denomination ministering to the lesbian and gay community.

In October of that year, he was diagnosed with AIDS, and as Christmas approached, he was hospitalized. Thirty children from a black Baptist church in San Francisco showed up at the hospital to sing carols for Clover and other persons with AIDS (PWAs). In the ensuing months, he was able to bring together the congregations of Double Rock Baptist Church, which condemns homosexuality as a sin, and MCC San Fran-

163

cisco, which preaches that homosexuality is a gift from God. These seemingly irreconcilable churches sponsored such events as a gospel music concert that raised more than one thousand dollars for the San Francisco AIDS Foundation Food Bank in July, 1987. Clover died a month later.

Clover's church is our church, MCC San Francisco, which is encircled by San Francisco's biggest gay and lesbian neighborhood. In many ways, Clover's story is our story. What he and others experienced individually, we undergo on an institutional level. We believe our drama has an impact on the larger body of the whole Christian community, especially churches in transition and those whose members include parents, relatives, and friends of PWAs.

Clover was a person with AIDS, like about twenty other PWAs in our congregation of about four hundred when he died in August, 1987. Currently, we know of about forty congregants who have been diagnosed with AIDS, and the number threatens to keep rising. About two-thirds of the men in the congregation are HIV positive, a sign they have been infected by the AIDS virus. Every week our worship service attracts at least one person who was just diagnosed. Death also attends weekly; the death of a member or a member's friend. Moreover, we perform several memorial services a month for people with AIDS who never set foot in our church. Their friends and the relatives, who come from churches all across America, turn to us because they know we will welcome them, honor gay relationships, and provide acceptance they cannot expect from most mainline churches.

Just as our members with AIDS suffer discrimination in housing, employment, and medical care, our church also suffers anti-AIDS discrimination in institutional forms. For example, a Roman Catholic retreat center said we could not use its facility unless we informed other groups that PWAs would be there. We regard this as denying us equal access. For the retreat center, the bottom line was the presence of PWAs in our group. "And what about the bathrooms?" the center coordinator persisted, revealing her ignorance of how AIDS is spread.

A CHURCH WITH AIDS

We have come to understand ourselves as a church with AIDS. This doesn't mean our church will soon be dead and gone. No; in fact, it means we live more deeply. The whole gay community is undergoing a parallel transformation. A lifestyle characterized by carefree promiscuity has given way to dating and friendship. Many people seek intimacy and spirituality, which has had the effect of a revival. Thus, despite the deaths of many members, our church's membership has actually grown by a third in the last year.

The Universal Fellowship of Metropolitan Community Churches (UFMCC) was founded in Los Angeles in 1968 by the Rev. Troy Perry, a former Pentecostal minister who aimed to spread the new gospel that God loves gays and lesbians. "All we had time to do was to celebrate and to grow," recalled the Rev. Howard Wells, speaking at our church a few years before he died of AIDS in September 1989. Wells founded MCC San Francisco in 1969. Grow we did: today there are more than thirty thousand MCC members in more than two hundred churches worldwide. But our innocent sense of celebration has died of AIDS. Wells said we now live with the end in sight, a state he called "eschatological living."

"The specter of AIDS catapults us into accelerated spiritual growth, or toward early death, and it all depends on the model of eschatological living we choose to follow," he said. On good days, being a church with AIDS helps us see how fragile and important every moment is. We rediscover images, such as heaven, that we used to dismiss as anachronistic or overly sentimental. We claim for ourselves the model described in scripture as "the realm of God," which Wells defined as "an alternative way of living."

It's not easy. We suffer the stages of grief on a grand scale, as we ricochet over and over again through denial, anger, bargaining, depression, and acceptance. Long-range planning is difficult for the church, just as it is for PWAs who are overwhelmed by having to make plans about wills, medical care, and finances. And yet planning has never been more crucial. Promoting church growth feels almost macabre, but without it we cannot meet the challenges ahead.

Sunday worship is typically marked by tears, laughter, and unforgettable singing. One of our favorite hymns was written by UFMCC members Jack Hoggatt-St. John and David Pelletier in 1980, before we were aware of AIDS: "We are the church alive, the body must be healed; where strife has bruised and battered us, God's wholeness is revealed" [ch. 13, p. 204]. Like Clover, we find that our struggle with AIDS has brought us insight into what it means to build heaven into our everyday lives, to try to realize the "realm of heaven" here and now.

Most of what our church has done concretely is in worship, peer support groups, education, and counseling. In each area, congregants work together with the pastor, who devotes about half his time to AIDS-related activities. These programs are coordinated by the AIDS ministry team, made up of about twenty congregants. In addition, we make our building available to dozens of AIDS-related groups.

We have tried different formats to meet the worship needs of our unique congregation. The monthly AIDS healing service began as an intimate, intense gathering where fifteen to twenty people affected by AIDS requested and received laying-on-of-hands prayer from each other. To listen to their stories is to enter into the enormity that is AIDS: A doctor sobs over his inability to heal his best friend. Someone who recently tested HIV positive confesses that his anger has separated him from his friends and his God. A withered man prays simply for an appetite. Another PWA proudly proclaims he is "living with AIDS, not dying of it." A nurse who has jabbed herself with an AIDS-contaminated needle says she feels numb now that ten of her co-workers have died of AIDS. The overall spirit was summed up by the son of a Lutheran minister: "Lutheran churches everywhere are dying—but this church isn't." In the past three years, the service has grown to encompass nearly two hundred worshipers, who mix their healing prayers with hymns of praise such as "When We All Get to Heaven." This service includes people from many other congregations, including regular participants from local Nazarene and Swedenborgian churches. We also hold special services, such as AIDS prayer vigils and the blessing of banners for the Names Project quilt that was part of the Lesbian and Gay Rights March on Washington in October, 1987. The quilt has toured many U.S. cities.

In a sense, all of our worship services are AIDS healing services. Every Sunday we provide a gay-positive, gay-affirming environment, where scripture is related to lesbian and gay experience and same-sex pairs can receive communion and laying-on-of-hands prayer as a couple. Our very existence refutes the often-held Christian position that AIDS is God's punishment for the sin of homosexuality, a position that breeds a self-hatred that many of us still struggle to overcome. Recently a young man confessed to the pastor before church that, under parental pressure, he had vowed sexual abstinence if God would cure him of AIDS—a typical response and one that reveals the heart of gay self-hatred.

Community prayer is the phase of Sunday worship when the impact of AIDS is most tangible. We join hands and share words and phrases that crystallize our concerns and joys. Every month we hear more petitions for "my friend who was just diagnosed" or "my lover in the hospital" or "more government funding for AIDS research" or "help me with my diagnosis."

AIDS-RELATED COUNSELING

Peer support groups provide a spiritual context for people to discuss what they have in common; in this case, a life-threatening illness, an HIV-positive condition, or being a caregiver to a PWA. In addition to these groups that are directly related to AIDS, our men's retreats and Men Together discussion/worship series approach the subject indirectly by encouraging men to make and deepen friendships away from bars, the traditional gay men's meeting ground. All of these become opportunities for dealing with AIDS-related grief. For example, at their spring 1987 retreat the men wrote, read, and discussed their experiences of touching other men. One of the readings discussed was this:

"Scott and I spent hard and precious times together from the time he was diagnosed with AIDS in 1983 until he died in 1984. . . . I was at work one day—my great escape from the illness was work—when I suddenly felt the need to be at home. . . . I laid with Scott, all the while telling him how much I loved him. I mentioned every person I could think of and made sure he heard that they loved him as well. Scott's labored breathing continued, with long lapses between breaths. Each lapse, I thought, would be his last. At 4:42, Scott's breathing stopped and never began again. I held him in my arms and softly told him again and again how precious he was. We spent forty-five minutes alone, with Scott in my arms for the last time. His body grew cold before I was finally able to release my hold on him. That most precious touch was to be our last.''

People turn to us for counseling at every stage of the AIDS crisis. Most of this is handled by clergy with support from student clergy and the AIDS ministry team. Touching is one of the most important ingredients in all 'AIDS counseling. Although AIDS cannot be spread through casual contact, PWAs tend to be treated as untouchables, which adds to their pain.

A congregant's first AIDS-related counseling often revolves around being tested for AIDS antibodies; a positive result means a person can transmit the AIDS virus and may develop AIDS himself or herself. Just deciding to take the test is excruciating. Even those who imagined they were prepared to face a positive result are often devastated by feelings of grief, guilt, and betrayal when the verdict is presented.

AIDS-related counseling also means home and hospital visitation, funerals, memorial services, and bereavement support. An unforgettable example occurred in summer, 1987, when one of us visited an AIDS hospice to take communion to a member, his parents, who were visiting from the east coast, and a few close friends. The man, obviously near death, urged everyone to pray not just for him, but for their own needs—a reversal of the angry response he expressed earlier in his illness. "I can see heaven," he told them. "It's a beautiful place, the place you've always wanted to go, and anyone who wants to can go there." The boundaries of heaven and earth seemed to shift that afternoon, so that they no longer corresponded to birth and death. It felt possible to reach into the skies and tug heaven into the present. Death became "a foretaste of the feast to come."

The man died a few hours later. His mother spoke at his memorial service, with tears in her eyes: "He was the best son a mother could ever have." And yet, she and her husband dreaded going back to their home church because they were reluctant to tell anyone in their United Methodist church that their son had died of AIDS. They didn't think anyone there would understand.

Another set of parents, also United Methodists, asked one of us to come to their son's hospital bedside to join them in prayer. There, the mother asked him, "Why are people so mean?" She was referring to unsympathetic church members back home. Their next question was even harder: Was it OK to pray for their comatose son to die soon? The whole church is coming to see that physical death is not necessarily something to avoid; it can even mean healing.

AIDS EDUCATION

AIDS education occurs in every setting we've described, as well as some programs whose main purpose is to educate. We declared September, 1987, AIDS education month, and brought in experts for a four-part series of forums on medical, emotional, and bereavement issues. An AIDS Foundation expert addressed MCC San Francisco women about possible lesbian transmission of the disease. Our shelf of free pamphlets is dominated by those about AIDS, which range from basic data on the disease to invitations for safe-sex workshops. People call our office so often for referrals to AIDS agencies that we sometimes feel like an AIDS information clearinghouse.

MCC San Francisco also strives to educate people outside our community about AIDS, through letter-writing campaigns, public presentations, and workshops on AIDS, which have been given in a variety of settings, including the San Francisco AIDS Interfaith Conference, the United Methodist Consultation on AIDS Ministries, the Presbyterian Ministers Association, and Pacific School of Religion's AIDS Awareness Week. In addition, MCC San Francisco members enrolled in the Pacific School of Religion continually pressure the seminary to live up to its policy on fair treatment of students with AIDS. Joint activities with Double Rock Baptist Church have been educational too. While we had to confront our own racism, the Baptists have had to surmount unfounded fears about catching AIDS. One Double Rock usher described holding hands with gay people during prayer time as "the most growing I have ever done."

In our church, AIDS has also brought reconciliation between the sexes, a rift that has been especially deep between lesbians and gay men. Like other women, lesbians face economic disadvantages. But in the case of lesbians, their resulting anger at men is untempered by romantic involvement with the opposite sex. Many lesbian feminists feel it is a waste of their energy to spend it in the traditional female role of helping men, their oppressors. However, that feeling doesn't prevail in our church. The topic of lesbians ministering to men with AIDS came up during a reception that the women of our church held for Rev. Karen Ziegler, then pastor of MCC New York. Ziegler responded this way: "I don't feel like I'm sacrificing;

I *receive* energy by ministering to men with AIDS."
She told us how "some men I love very much—my
friends David and Tim—began to die of AIDS. I had
the experience of coming closer than I ever had come
to a man before. David, and then Tim, opened a door
to their souls in a way that I had never experienced
before, and my heart has been opened in a way it
never was before, too. We're all experiencing that
transformation together." This issue has also been
mitigated by a small but growing number of women
with AIDS in our congregation.

We have also connected with Congregation Sha'ar
Zahav, a Reform synagogue with a lesbian and gay congregation, located a few blocks from our church. Together we sponsored a reading by award-winning
lesbian poet Adrienne Rich. That evening, Rich told
us, "Lesbians and gay men have confronted mortality.
We have mourned our friends and lovers together and
we have stitched an extraordinary quilt of memory together. . . . I think that the coming together of Jewish
and Christian, lesbian and gay and straight congregants
is an important part of this. I also think that the coming
together of those of us who are non-congregants with
you is very important."

The National Council of Churches' Commission on
Faith and Order attended one of our healing services,
called "We Are the Body of Christ and We Have
AIDS" in March, 1989 [ch. 1, p. 35]. More than fifty
commissioners jammed themselves into the already
crowded sanctuary for the worship experience of their
lives. Expecting a mournful mood, they were taken
aback by the rainbow flags, balloons, and jubilant singing. One commissioner testified, "You sing like you've
already gone to heaven!" Although MCC San Francisco generally shares the eucharist at every worship
service, we refrained that night in deference to NCC

custom. (The only time the NCC has ever had communion together was several years before, also at MCC San Francisco, as part of their consideration of UFMCC's membership application, which was later tabled permanently.)

Some of our congregants were offended by this omission and wondered if it was because we are lesbian and gay. We explained that it wasn't that the NCC didn't want to share communion with us; rather, they didn't want to share it with each other. Commissioner Jeane Audrey Powers apologized by saying, "MCC, you are teaching us what it means to be the church." AIDS has taught us that the differences that divide churches are trivial in the face of the enormous challenges and blessings that AIDS presents. AIDS has shown us how much we need the church, and AIDS is showing the larger church that they need everyone. God calls the church to challenge the status quo, not reinforce it. Our church is a present glimpse of a future time when all will be welcome at God's table [ch. 4, p. 77].

This kind of connection—between Jew and Christian, female and male, gay and straight, black and white, parent and child—is what eschatological living is all about. With the end in sight, we do more to savor and value life, including the people we once viewed as hopelessly different from ourselves. As a church with AIDS, we try to embody eschatological living. AIDS is killing us at the same time that it heals us.

This must be the vision Clover was talking about when he told us, "Heaven has as much to do with life before death as with life after death."

This must be the vision Rich meant to convey when she wrote the poem that has become a kind of creed for our church:

My heart is moved by all I cannot save:
so much has been destroyed

I have to cast my lot with those
who age after age, perversely,

with no extraordinary power,
reconstitute the world.[1]

This must be what Jesus meant when he said, "Behold, the kingdom of God is in the midst of you."

12 *Katharine Doob Sakenfeld*

Who Is My Neighbor?

Jesus' story of the good Samaritan, recounted in Luke 10:25–37, is surely among the best known of New Testament passages. From my earliest years in Sunday school, I knew from this story that Jesus wanted all people, even children, to be kind to strangers and outsiders, not just to those who were members of our own group. When I was a teenager growing up in the South, this story helped shape my perspective on race relations. It has continued to be important to me as I have recognized more and more ways in which most of us on this planet manage to marginalize each other and, in effect, declare one another beyond the bounds of neighborly responsibility.

But the familiar story of the good Samaritan has taken on new power as communities of people concerned about the AIDS crisis have shared their reflections on it with me. Fresh dimensions and possibilities for hearing the story have multiplied in our conversations; this chapter gathers together some of those reflections, organized around these six questions:

> Why was the traveler on the road?
> How did the traveler end up in the ditch?
> What are the questions the Samaritan did
>   not ask?

Who is the Samaritan in our context?
How can the Jericho road be made safer?
How does the story of the Samaritan call us
     to respond?

WHY WAS THE TRAVELER ON THE ROAD?

It is probably safe to assume that Jesus was not interested in the answer to this question. Jesus was focusing on how and by whom a person injured on the road was rescued and healed. So why should we ask this question? Precisely to put ourselves on notice that the answer was not of interest to Jesus. We ourselves, to the contrary, tend to be very interested in such questions. News reports of travel accidents always seem to include information about the purpose of the journey, whether it was grocery shopping, visiting relatives, business, or vacation. And when trouble occurs, we have the habit of measuring out our sympathy, our desire to help, in proportion to how we evaluate the source of the trouble. So we denigrate the plight of the injured traveler in the biblical story by thinking that he ought not to have been on such a dangerous road, that he should not have been so foolish as to travel alone, that his business could not have been so urgent.

And so it is with AIDS. If the person living with AIDS is represented for us by the injured person along the Jericho road, many of us are inordinately curious about how it happened that the person first became HIV positive. Of course, such information is needed for research and for prevention, but all too often we tend to use it to rank the worthiness of these persons as candidates for medical care, for our friendship, or even for God's love. The claim made by some that AIDS is divine punishment of particular individuals for their I.V. drug use or for a certain kind of sexual practice represents the worst of such ranking and should be rejected. But even those of us who find ourselves with greater sympathy for a person who contracts AIDS by blood transfusion than for one who contracts AIDS through sexual contact are asking the question Jesus didn't ask: Why was the traveler on the road? The biblical story challenges us, both as individuals and as church and world communities, to set aside our categorizing and our tendency to blame the victim, and to get on with the task of helping the needy [ch. 11, p. 173].

How Did the Traveler End Up in the Ditch?

To be sure, the biblical text does not specify a ditch, or even exactly where in relation to the road the wounded man lay. "The ditch" here is simply shorthand for the condition of the traveler: stripped, beaten, and left half dead. In the biblical story, the man is the victim of robbers who fell upon him. Again, we must beware of our tendency to blame the victim for his plight when we note that the road from Jerusalem to Jericho was well-known for its danger to travelers. Again, it is safe to say that Jesus did not concentrate on this part of the story; it serves as prelude to reporting of actions of the priest, the Levite, and the Samaritan as three passers-by who see the wounded man. Before we rush to identify ourselves with one (or more) of these four main characters, however, it may be helpful to think about ourselves in relation to those robbers, the one set of characters we tend to pass over in this story. In what circumstances in relation to AIDS might some of us need to think of ourselves as perpetrators such as these, rather than as those who have an opportunity to assist in time of need? Conversation around this question might refer to the transmission of the virus, with a suggestion that those few persons who know they are infected and deliberately fail to take precautions concerning their body fluids are like the robbers falling upon a victim. More generally, and more important, however, all of us, individually and especially as the church seeking unity and renewal, need to consider how we may be making the AIDS crisis worse in some active way, not just "passing by on the other side" and ignoring it. For example, failure to become informed, and especially perpetuating falsehoods (such as that AIDS is a "gay" disease, or that it is transmitted by mosquitoes), leads not only to more cases of AIDS but also to the destructive dehumanization of those living with AIDS [ch. 10, p. 149]. Such behavior is frighteningly similar to that of the robbers in the Samaritan story, and we must strive to avoid it and even to counteract it.

WHAT ARE THE QUESTIONS THE SAMARITAN DID NOT ASK?

The biblical story states only that when the Samaritan saw the beaten man, "he had compassion, and went to him." Whatever the Samaritan may have wondered to himself, he asked no questions at all in the course of his acts of caring. He did not ask why the man was on the road or why he traveled alone. He did not ask about the man's "medical coverage," his ability to pay for medication or bedside care. He did not ask who else could help. He did not ask how long the period of care by the innkeeper would be. He helped without asking whether the robbers were still lurking nearby, ready to fall upon him also. In short, the Samaritan represents for us the biblical definition of the true neighbor precisely because he did not ask any of the questions or make any of the excuses that we normally make. With AIDS, especially, our excuses tend to be manifold, perhaps because of the magnitude of the problem. The Samaritan invites individuals and the church to live differently, for the sake of the world [ch. 6, pp. 100–103; ch. 13, pp. 183–195].

WHO IS THE SAMARITAN IN THE CONTEXT OF AIDS?

The easy answer to this question, the one that surfaces quickly, is that the person or group who comes to the support (personal, emotional, financial, medical) of those with AIDS is like the Samaritan. The hidden assumption in this answer is generally that the Samaritan's role is played by those who do not have AIDS. Yet as soon as this is stated explicitly, the fallacy of this assumption becomes apparent. For in many situations it is in fact those living with AIDS who are the most active in support of others in the same situation [ch. 11, pp. 163–164]. Furthermore, if we take seriously the central point of Jesus' story, it is precisely the despised and outcast Samaritan who demonstrates to everyone the true meaning of being neighbor. From this point of view, the Samaritan suddenly may become those who have AIDS helping those who do not to deal with their fears or hatred; the person lying beaten along the road may be any of us. In the context of the church, the example of the ministry of the Metropolitan Community Churches in this crisis may be a special instance of the role of the Samaritan, as a group of Christians often ignored and even openly rejected seek to carry out a ministry of healing and reconciliation.

Church people involved in AIDS ministries emphasize that one of their greatest challenges is to break through the we-they mentality that permeates our thinking about this crisis. Those who do not have AIDS tend to speak of themselves as "we" and speak of those who have AIDS as "they." A careful answer to the question of who is the Samaritan suggests that, from a Christian perspective, no stereotypical formulation of we-they is appropriate. As those active in AIDS ministries have put it, we *all* need to come to grips with the reality that "*we* have AIDS"; that we all need healing [ch. 1, p. 41].

While the responses to the first three questions above are structured around an implicit assumption that the man attacked by robbers represents persons with AIDS, the multiple answers to this fourth question show us that this is not the only approach to finding ourselves in the story. We see that if "*we* have AIDS," then healing encompasses far more than helping those whom the medical profession classifies as "having AIDS." The wounded one lying on the road may be any of us. Furthermore, in reflecting on the previous questions, we must include persons with AIDS in our thinking about the role of the Samaritan. The paragraphs above are written to be open to that possibility, and you are encouraged to reread them with new eyes if that has not occurred to you. As we overcome the we-they mentality, we all, individually and corporately, will have a greater possibility both of receiving healing and of being the Samaritan, if only we are able to choose it.

How Can the Jericho Road Be Made Safer?

Again, we are asking a question that was not pertinent to the immediate point of Jesus' story about the Samaritan. But the question of preventing or at least reducing the continuing scandal of attacks along the road comes up as often as the story is discussed. It is appropriate to the story in the context of scripture as a whole, for the overall biblical witness is concerned for transformation of social structure as "preventive care" to reduce the number of wounded persons. The need for systemic change is glaringly apparent in many arenas of life. It is here that the corporate character of the church becomes especially significant, and where we can see the importance of unity and renewal of both church and human community. The church will truly be the church as it seeks to make the road safe, to do justice for the sake of the world [ch. 9, p. 145].

In the responses to each of the previous questions, there is the possibility of viewing all the Samaritan story characters as representative of groups rather than of individuals. The response to the present question does not focus directly on any of the story characters, but the group or communal concern present throughout the discussion comes into especially sharp focus. With regard to AIDS, it seems clear that individual acts of caring are not sufficient, in themselves, to meet the national and global crisis. Education, research, and affordable treatment all require concern and commitment from large groups of people with diverse experience and background, and specialized skills. Examples from all across the United States testify to ways in which the AIDS crisis has led to new levels of cooperation as Christians from different backgrounds seek to respond together. Perhaps from the seed of such local and regional action will sprout the tender shoot of unity and renewal among people of faith. The church marked by holiness and set in an inescapably interdependent universe will, more and more, seek to transform structures for the good of all people [ch. 5, p. 79]. And such change in the church may, by God's grace, be catalytic for change in the world.

HOW DOES THE STORY OF THE SAMARITAN CALL US TO RESPOND?

The answers to this concluding question summarize what has been said in response to the first five. The list can only be a beginning, and certainly will not be exhaustive. Readers are invited to add to these suggestions.

All of us—individually, as the church, and by God's grace as one world—need to come to understand that "*we* have AIDS."

We need individually and corporately to understand that in different aspects of our lives, with regard to AIDS, we probably play several of the roles in this story, victim as well as Samaritan, robber as well as priest or Levite.

Recognizing these multiple roles in the context of the knowledge that *we* have AIDS, all of us need to seek healing and all of us need to seek forgiveness.

> We need to stop ignoring the issue.
> We need to stop asking inappropriate
>   questions.
> We need to stop making excuses.
> We need to stop perpetuating ignorance and
>   falsehood.
> We need to work for systemic change that
>   will reduce both illness and dehumaniza-
>   tion associated with AIDS, thus striving to
>   "make the road safe."

Faced with the brokenness represented by AIDS, we need to recommit ourselves as Christians to the vision of a unified and renewed church and human community, for it is this vision which is the ultimate ground for insisting that *we* have AIDS.

13   *J. Shannon Clarkson, editor*

Resources for Study and Action

CHURCH RESPONSES TO AIDS

Southern Baptist Churches*

As an agent of healing and fountain of compassion, the church has often failed to respond to persons with AIDS (PWAs) with healing and compassion. Many Southern Baptist churches are still in denial that AIDS has come to the church. The urgency of the need to minister to PWAs is perhaps surpassed only by the unavoidable fact of the rapidly spreading nature of the disease. Few congregations remain untouched by this modern-day plague. Writes Richard Schaper,

> [T]he church, however, cannot and need not wait to reach consensus on homosexuality before addressing the staggering spiritual needs of those who are ill with AIDS. Surely, a stricken human being need not be of a certain sexual orientation in order to qualify for the compassion of Christ and the church . . . reaching out in mercy to someone with AIDS implies more about the faith of the church than it does about the morality or immorality of the sufferer.[1]

*R. Page Fulgham

William E. Amos, Jr., is pastor of the First Baptist Church of Plantation, Florida. In his attempt to minister to his church, to persons with AIDS and to their families, he educated himself, and faced "AIDS hysteria" and homophobia while continuing to minister with Christ's compassion. By his openness and honesty in the pulpit and in person-to-person contact, Amos has enabled many to deal with the disease. In his book, *When AIDS Comes to Church,* Amos writes,

> The church does not need to abandon its prophetic role in society. It does not need to abdicate its concern with lifestyle choices and behaviors which result in people becoming less than God intended for them. However, as we struggle with this, the biblical record is clear that our identity is as ministers of reconciliation. . . . In Christ, God accepts us as we are with all our sins and shortcomings, whatever their nature. Out of that relationship of acceptance, Christ then calls us to belong to him and live for him.[2]

As a positive response to the AIDS crisis, Bill Amos outlines a model program for the church. His suggestions include referring with compassion to AIDS issues from the pulpit; congregational involvement by equipping the membership for ministry; educating the community about AIDS; establishing policies for the church nursery reflecting a thorough study of the subject, the underlying issue of sexual behavior, and a Christlike compassion; the establishment of support groups for AIDS patients and their families; hospice care and a prayer group for persons with AIDS.

A leader among churches working with PWAs in Atlanta is the Northside Drive Baptist Church, where Thomas H. Conley is senior pastor. Conley stated in an interview that his church's involvement in the AIDS crisis includes a pulpit ministry centered around compassionate concern in a non-judgmental way. Rev. Conley said he separates the disease from the gay lifestyle and simply ministers to persons in need. The Northside church is supportive of AID Atlanta, an advocacy and care group that provides education, support, and hospice care for PWAs and their families.

In recent years, the congregation has ministered to approximately twenty-four families, many of whom lost family members to AIDS. Much educational work has been accomplished with pastors whose members were part of the Atlanta community and who contracted the disease. Associate Pastor Joan Pritcher serves as chaplain in the pastoral care department of AID Atlanta. Rev. Conley is also actively involved in lobbying in the state legislature for nondiscriminatory laws for PWAs.

Travis Berry, director of church relations for Baylor Health Care System in Dallas, Texas, suggests that each church form an AIDS resource committee composed of health-care professionals and laypersons. The tasks of this committee would include recommending AIDS-related church policies for nursery care, worship, and ministry. He encourages open dialogue within the church and the creation of an educational program that will provide clear, accurate information about the threat of AIDS and its transmission. Berry believes that facts about transmission of the AIDS virus will quell fears of Southern Baptists who are called to minister.

"Giving help to people in need," says Berry, "should not depend on our approving everything about them. If people are going to die they ought not need the Good Housekeeping seal of approval."[3]

The Christian Life Commission of the Baptist Convention of Texas has published an AIDS resource packet that includes facts about AIDS, a theological approach to AIDS, and recommendations for action. Suggestions for practical ministry include personal ministry to persons with AIDS and their families, education of church members about AIDS, and creation of health awareness in Sunday schools and day-care facilities.

At a recent meeting on AIDS, a Southern Baptist pastor said the AIDS crisis touches every major taboo we have.

> Our ability to deal effectively with this crisis means we must face such sensitive issues as sex education for youth, promiscuity of youth and adults, general AIDS education, homosexuality, drug abuse, death and dying, grief and ministry to those who have been rejected by society.[4]

This brief sample of representative Southern Baptist approaches to the AIDS crisis reveals that not all Southern Baptists have their heads in the sand. Yet the great silent majority remains silent. Perhaps Ronald Sider provides a voice for what is not being said:

> How should Christians respond to people with AIDS? Our Christian understanding of both creation and redemption tells us that people with AIDS are of inestimable worth, persons so important and precious in the sight of their creator and redeemer that God declares them indelibly stamped with the divine image. Indeed, people with AIDS are so special that the creator of the galaxies declares that his son's death on the cross was precisely for them. No matter how weak or frail, no matter how marginalized or despised, no matter how ravaged by wrong choices, people with AIDS enjoy full sanctity of human life. So we offer them our love and support, no matter how inconvenient or costly. That is the first, middle, and last thing to say.[5]

Theological Statement Developed by the Union of Black Episcopalians' AIDS Task Force*

"The wrath of God." How often we have heard that phrase, or even said it. Most of us who have uttered it

*Nan Arrington Peete, primary author

have paid little attention to its meaning or implication. However, we are now confronted with it in regards to the AIDS disease and crisis in our communities.

As Christians, our faith comes from a loving and compassionate God, as manifested through Jesus Christ, who gave us a new commandment: "Love one another, as I have loved you." Therefore, we are called to respond in love to the AIDS crisis. This raises many issues for us in the black community. Therefore, the UBEAT presents its theological understanding of its mission.

AIDS is not "the wrath of God" upon homosexuals. AIDS is a human disease that can and does afflict all groups of people in our society. After the flood, God told Noah, "Never again will I inflict disaster upon my people." This is the only unconditional covenant that God makes with us. Disease is not a tool of God. If it were, then cancer, sickle-cell anemia, and heart attacks could also be considered God's wrath. As you can see, we can take this to absurdity. God does not use illness against us. In the Gospel of John, Jesus' disciples asked him about the man born blind. They asked, "Was he born blind because he sinned, or his parents?" Jesus responds, "It was not that this man sinned, or his parents, but that the works of God might be made manifest in him." The disciples were astonished, God was, and is, giving us an opportunity to heal each other and to love each other. Illness and disease are not limited to certain people or certain groups of people. We have been given an opportunity to show God's love manifested in us, as we minister to those with AIDS.

God is not a punishing, vengeful God. God so loved the world that he gave his only begotten Son. Jesus came into a world full of corruption, injustice, and malice—yet a world still loved by God, the world God created and said "was good" and "is good."

Love without limits. "I give you a new commandment: love one another, as I have loved you." There are no qualifiers or conditional phrases in that statement. Jesus does not limit who we are to love. We are called to embrace the prodigal child, without knowing about the child's repentance; we are called to love the Samaritan woman whom no one would speak to or, in our world, the AIDS patient who may have been abandoned by his or her family, friends, or colleagues. This love is unconditional. God's unconditional love for us is not earned or deserved, but given graciously and freely by God to all of us.

This love we have for each other, while unconditional, carries some challenges and responsibilities for us. How do we live this love in the context of our sexuality and the ethical issues raised by AIDS? The sexuality issue is broader and more complex than just the issue of homosexuality. It includes our acknowledgment and understanding of the intrinsic good in sexual relationships. This unconditional love we have for each other also calls us to respond to the issue of I.V. drug use. We can no longer say, "I won't support providing clean needles because it would mean that I am condoning drug use"; the alternative is the extraordinary costs, both medical and nonmedical, of caring for children born with AIDS. It means that we must make every effort to reach drug users and share with them accurate information, and resources, and the help they need. We must also spend time, money, and effort in eliminating the root causes of addiction.

Sex education for young adults is critical in the black community. If we truly care about the next generation, we must begin to see that they have accurate information about their bodies and the impact of sexual activity. AIDS, teenage pregnancy, and absent fathers all stem from the lack of adequate sex education information. We must no longer live under the false assumptions that not talking about sex, or not having sex, or what they don't know won't hurt them; or that if we provide them with sex education and provide them with resources, then they will become sexually active and we are condoning sexual activity. Young people need this information to make responsible decisions about their bodies and their lives. We must not abdicate our role. The fastest growing age group of those getting AIDS is the teenage group.

The church has said that having children is no longer the sole basis for sexual intercourse in marriage. That means that sexual intercourse, in and of itself, is intrinsically good. The issue then becomes: What are the criteria or conditions for sexual intercourse between two people? Is it the state-issued marriage license? Is it only good between certain people? Are sequential sexual partners, as found in a succession of marriages, better than a long-term loving relationship outside of marriage? If children are no longer the sole reason for sexual relations, then why do we not acknowledge same-sex relations?

Disease is not a tool of God. We are made in the image of God, male and female, and our bodies are the temple of God. We should not abuse them. Yet all of us do, with food, alcohol, smoking, improper—or lack of—exercise, drugs, and sex. Promiscuity as a way of life is inappropriate for anyone. How we treat ourselves, and our bodies, is an indication of how we feel about God. Likewise, how we see others' bodies is an indication of the respect we have for them and for God. All of us are made in the image of God. Therefore, God is in those persons with AIDS as well. How we reach out to them also reflects how we reach out to God.

We as black Episcopalians have an opportunity to make manifest the works of God in our response to the AIDS crisis in our community. We can no longer say that the disease does not affect me or my family or my neighbor. We are all related. What affects one part of the body, affects all parts. Just as South Africa is the *kairos* place where the justice of God is being made manifest, so is the AIDS crisis the *kairos* time and place where the love of God is made manifest.

Universal Fellowship of Metropolitan Community Churches*

When the Faith, Fellowship, and Order (FFO) commission of the Universal Fellowship of Metropolitan Community Churches convened its 1986 meeting at MCC-Dallas, Texas, AIDS was the top priority on the agenda. The theological commission of UFMCC decided to spend a full day discussing how AIDS is affecting our work as a commission and our lives as gay and lesbian Christians. The commission is composed of elected lay and clergy representatives from each MCC district, plus Hispanic and black representatives, and more than twenty-five people were present from Denmark, Canada, and the United States. The meeting represented both a genuine cross section of MCC, and the FFO commission's official response to the National Council of Churches' Commission on Faith and Order, which is using this information as part of a case study on "AIDS, Homophobia, and the Church" commissioned by its Unity of the Church and Renewal of Human Community study group.

At the meeting, a brief poll was taken of the levels of involvement in AIDS-related activities and the disease itself in the group, including plans for the MCC's 1989

*Jennie Boyd Bull

fall "AIDS Vigil of Prayer"; participation in the FFO commission's Lenten study series on AIDS, "Do Not Fear, Only Believe"; local congregational AIDS ministry; personal AIDS ministry; and of personal involvement with the disease. Involvement was extremely high (75–80 percent), with three persons working full time in AIDS ministry and two persons with spouses diagnosed with AIDS. The commission spent time in small groups, sharing personal experiences and answering the four questions that follow. (These questions were proposed by the NCC Commission on Faith and Order study, based on an action-reflection model, and adapted for the FFO commission's use.) Each small group reported to the whole on their discussion, and general consensus statements were drawn up for each question. The chair then transcribed these notes into the text that appears here, in abbreviated form.

1. What are the crucial issues for human renewal that the FFO commission was designed to address and how have these changed in response to AIDS?

The FFO commission was formed around the following goals: (1) recognition of a split between mind and body, spirituality and sexuality, in our culture and in Christianity, and a need to heal that brokenness in embodied wholeness, the "embodiment" of God in *all* of us in mind, body, and spirit; (2) continued growth toward self-acceptance as gays and lesbians—toward a sex-positive attitude in the face of the culture's sex negativity and homophobia (the fear of homosexuality); (3) building consensus for the UFMCC's statement of faith, from an ecumenical perspective; and (4) empowering the laity through a commission of lay-clergy parity, as "the priesthood of all believers" wherein "we are all theologians."

Changes in these issues within the UFMCC in response to AIDS have primarily been that they have become much more intense, more real, and more personal. Issues of sexuality, of embodiment, and of homophobia are all heightened by the AIDS crisis. Part of dealing with that homophobia has been facing the specific question of AIDS and God's judgment and writing a statement in response: the 1985 FFO brochure, "Is AIDS God's Judgment? A Christian View of Faith, Hope and Love from Metropolitan Community Church." The other major change is an increased focus on questions of evil, suffering, and death, and an affirmation of resurrection, healing, and life in response. There is a profound sense of spiritual strength and of deepening and affirmation of faith and life.

2. What were the theological or faith assumptions operative in the FFO commission's formation, and how have these changed in response to AIDS?

Certain theological assumptions reflect MCC's role as an ecumenical church with a ministry in the gay and lesbian community. One assumption is that sexuality is a gift of God and that homosexuality is not sinful. Other assumptions relate to process: Theology is based in experience as the primary source of revelation, supported by scripture and tradition; theology is a journey, a process, an evolving; theology assumes an acceptance of diversity: "Many paths, one faith in Christ."

Changes in these theological assumptions reflect the intensifying effect of AIDS. Theology must be relational, personalized; and worship, prayer, and praise are essential in "doing theology." The importance of the holistic health and healing movements has increased as these movements interact with our faith. There is also a perceived need for increased consensus and affirmation of our faith. Some at the meeting felt the need for a more concise faith statement. Others focused on "not wasting our time on disagreements" and "getting on with essentials." It was pointed out that in one sense, these changes are about living out the experiential, personal focus of the commission.

3. With what understanding or attitude toward the church did the FFO commission begin? What is that understanding or attitude now, and what about the AIDS crisis caused it to change or remain the same?

The FFO commission began with the understanding that "We are the church, we are the People of God," and it is about "articulating the experience of God moving through an oppressed people." The church's ministry is one of reconciliation and healing. The AIDS crisis has intensifed that bond. We have moved beyond a bonding around sexuality to a bonding around mortality, and claim resurrection, healing, and life in the face of evil, suffering, and death. Facing death has made us take ourselves more seriously as the church, and made us take more responsibility and undertake more activism in our community. Someone said, "We are the experts now; we are healing the physically and spiritually wounded of the other churches." Person after person testified about MCC's being sought out for its pastoral expertise in this crisis. Out of this comes an increased intensity and focus on the ministry of reconciliation and healing.

4. What church-dividing or -uniting issues have arisen in your work around AIDS, and how have you sought to address them?

Discussing this question was especially helpful, because some issues had not yet been clearly raised as sources of division, and of potential unity, as they are confronted and worked through. The interrelation of sin and sickness and their relationship with faith and

healing are primary issues which can divide congregations, and can involve everything from blaming and
judgmental attitudes to disillusionment when faithful
prayer does not result in physical healing. Issues of
sexual morality are divisive, and are rooted in internalized homophobia and horizontal violence (taking our
self-hatred out on one another). Division between gay
men, who are the highest risk group for AIDS, and lesbians, who are the lowest risk group, is an issue in
some congregations, with women especially fearful
that AIDS will one more time put the focus on men's
instead of women's concerns. It is also true that women
and men are learning to work together and support
each other across these differences in ways not possible before. AIDS is seen as both bringing greater conflict in our churches (in grief, fear, and stress reactions)
and as bringing greater commitment. The grief reactions of denial and anger bring conflict, but facing
death also brings commitment and faith.

Racism is a divisive issue in our congregations and
our communities. One person of color called this the
Cain syndrome—"You caused it." As increasing numbers of black people are diagnosed with AIDS, the lack
of outreach in the black community by MCC congregations increasingly is a stumbling block to ministry, but
it is also an incentive for greater involvement in those
communities. Another issue is increased awareness of
drug abuse and alcoholism in the gay community, and
the need to address directly these problems in response to AIDS. As one person pointed out, "More gays
die of alcoholism each year than they do of AIDS."

A more specific area of conflict is negotiating priorities for ministry in local congregations, as pastors and
laity spend an increasing amount of energy doing AIDS
work, in pastoral care, education, and advocacy, and
other issues receive less time. One comment was that

AIDS is intensifying the need to deal with ongoing community pastoral issues such as sexuality, drug use, alcoholism, racism, and sexism, but at times AIDS ministry can be perceived as taking away from ministry in these other areas. Others see AIDS ministry helping us deal more effectively with all of these issues.

Our responses to these diverse, dividing and uniting issues are hopeful. We strongly agree that we face death with deepening faith, and this faith helps us heal the divisions. The FFO commission is responding with resources for education and for increasing skills in the process of reconciliation. And this ministry, as with all new ministries, helps our church to grow, in maturity and faith as well as in numbers.

WORSHIP RESOURCES

Liturgy for Casting Out Fear

Call to Worship

We gather this day in the presence of God's outstretched arms—arms opened wide in comforting love and assurance.

> Oh that our arms might also be as widely open, rather than drawn back in fear and ignorance.

We gather this day in the presence of God's open hands—hands eager to touch each one of us.

> Oh that our hands might also be as freely offered—to lift and embrace our sister or brother with AIDS.

We gather this day in the presence of God's overwhelming love—which seeks not to question or judge, seeks not to rationalize or eulogize—but seeks to accept and empower with new life and hope.

Empower us in our time together, O God, to open
our minds, open our hearts, and freely open our
very selves to all who need a hug and the comforting, uplifting assurance of your presence. *The minister asks worshipers to turn to those persons
around them and exchange a few informal words of
greeting and a handshake or hug.*

Hymn *"Creator God, Creating Still"*   **ST. ANNE**
                                      Jane Parker Huber (alt.)[6]

Creator God, creating still, By will and word
    and deed,
Create a new humanity To meet the present
    need.
Redeemer God, redeeming still, With over-
    flowing grace,
Pour out your love on us, through us, Make
    this a holy place.

Sustainer God, sustaining still, With strength
    for every day,
Empower us now to do your will. Correct us
    when we stray.
Creator God, for this new day We need your
    presence still.
Create, redeem, sustain us now To do your
    work and will.

Confession in Unison
I see the face of AIDS
    in my world on every continent
        in my country in every state
    in my city in each neighborhood.

I see the face of AIDS,
    it is a face contorted in fear, a deep fear
        of blood
            of sex

of death
of homosexuals
fear of Africans and Haitians
 fear of people different from the self.

A plague in our times, in our family.
 Can you believe it?
  Terror in newspaper headlines
  national and municipal budgets stretched
   insurance companies unable to cope with the
    bills
   johns unwilling to use a condom for their illicit
    pleasure
    parents unable to control their children's sex-
    ual explorations
  Ignorance and fear mixed as thick as peanut
  butter.

I see the face of AIDS,
 it is a face thin, old, worn before its time
  eyes receding in their sockets
   staring beyond the thin veil of present reality
  seeing a life beyond and unsure of the route.

I see the face of AIDS
 in the quiet saint of our times
 who steps forward to care for this babe,
  for the mother,
  for all infected
 for as long as they shall live.

I see the face of AIDS
 in my neighbor who comes home from the hospital
   in an ambulance
 to the arms of his lover, who carries him into the
   house
  like a bride.
 They live out their lives in quiet retreat together

sleeping in the same bed
each terrified of going on alone.

I see the face of AIDS
    in the outraged crowd gathering to protest
        too high a price
        being charged for an elixir which offers hope to
            the hopeless.

I see the face of AIDS everywhere now on the streets of
            my world
    because I see it in myself
        one of the worried well.[7]

Assurance of Pardon and Thanksgiving   *(Psalm 118:1–4)*
O give thanks to the Lord for the Lord is good;
The Lord's steadfast love endures for ever!
Let Israel say,
    "The Lord's steadfast love endures for ever."
Let the house of Aaron say,
    "The Lord's steadfast love endures for ever."
Let those who fear the Lord say,
    "The Lord's steadfast love endures for ever."

Scripture   *Isaiah 40:27–31; 42:1–4; Revelation 21:1–4*

Litany
God of might and compassion, God of judgment and
forgiveness, God of creation and redemption; you
who have enabled us to be who we are and who have
nudged and beckoned us through all our days,

> We call upon you now on behalf of our sisters and
> brothers whose lives have been touched by the dis-
> ease we call AIDS.

We believe, Lord, that in ways beyond our ability to
fully comprehend, you intend for your people whole-

ness and health; that you would have us to be well in mind and body and spirit.

And yet we confess that we have not always sufficiently treasured the gift of personhood you have given.

We have depreciated your gift of life in ourselves and in others.

And you have called us to love one another.

Love, you said. Love. That doesn't mean we have to *like* one another or *agree* with one another or even *know* one another; just *love* one another.

And that's not easy, Lord.

We know that too many times we have been oblivious to the needs of others, treating others as strangers rather than as persons created in your image.

Some of us don't really know anyone with AIDS—and some do.

Some of us know families of persons with AIDS who have tried to keep their awful secret to themselves, silently afraid that rejection might be added to their burden of sorrow.

Some of us are those families.

And all of us are a fearful people, living in the midst of a fearful people.

And yet you are a God who has called us "not to fear what they fear."

And so we come now, humbling ourselves to ask your presence with us, with persons with AIDS and with their families.

Grant wisdom among those who search for ways of controlling or eradicating this disease.

Give to our political and religious leaders a true sense of responsible compassion, that they may encourage us and help us find the ways of being people of love.

Help those who have AIDS and their families to know your presence and support in affliction and not to judge illness a sign of your absence.

Hear our prayer, O Lord.

Amen.

Liturgy for Casting Out Stones

(You will receive a stone. During the moments that follow, reflect on the stone held in your hand—how it feels, how it can be used. Meditate on the stone imagery in scripture, and stone imagery in relation to our attitudes toward persons with AIDS.)

"Or what one of you, if your child asks for bread, will give a stone?"   *(Matt. 7:9, alt.)*

What is a stone, anyway? It is cold, hard, dirty, lifeless; covered with sharp edges.

This life of mine can sometimes be cold, hard, dirty and life-denying. This life of mine also has sharp, cutting edges. This life of mine can hurt and bring pain. Sometimes we are much like the stones we hold in our hands.

Forgive us, O God, when our only response to the outstretched arm of our neighbor with AIDS is a stone-cold hardness of heart, rather than a warm hug and free outpouring of love; a sharp, cutting remark, rather than words of compassion and hope.

Forgive us, O God, when we choose ignorance in hope of protecting a presumed childhood innocence rather than knowledge to help protect our lives. Forgive our nation, O God, for not quickly tipping our budgetary scale in favor of life: AIDS research, education, and much greater assistance to the AIDS patient, rather than the proliferation of instruments of death and destruction.

"For everything there is a season and a time for every matter under heaven . . . a time to cast away stones, and a time to gather stones together . . . a time to keep, and a time to cast away . . . "   *(Eccl. 3:1, 5, 6)*

. . . a time to clutch stones, and a time to cast them away. A time to clutch our fears, and a time to let go of our fears and walk in faith. Forgive us, O God, for firmly clutching the stones of ignorance and death rather than casting them from our lives—*now!*

"The stone which the builders rejected has become the head of the corner."   *(Ps. 118:22)*

Not all stones are instruments of hurt. That stone in your hand can be used to build a new foundation of love and understanding.

And, gathered together with the stones of others, my stone can pave the way toward greater love and understanding.

" 'Come now, let us make a covenant, you and I; and let it be a witness between you and me.' So Jacob took a stone, and set it up as a pillar. And Jacob said to his kinsmen, 'Gather stones,' and they took stones, and made a heap. . . . Then Laban said to Jacob, 'See this heap and the pillar, which I have set between you and me. This heap is a witness, and the pillar is a witness' " *(Gen. 31:44–46, 51–52)*. As Jacob took a stone and joined it with the stones of others to create a visible covenantal sign, let us join our stones with the stones of others in this room, as a sign of our covenant with one another to work and pray together on behalf of our brothers and sisters with AIDS.

Litany of Healing

O God, we come before you this day with longing, with hungering, with tremendous need of your healing presence. We pray on behalf of ourselves, our loved ones, our community, and our world.

Loving God, we receive your gentle, powerful, healing touch.

For people who have tested HIV positive and endure tension-filled waiting; sometimes hopeful and optimistic, sometimes frozen with fear and despair . . . (silent prayer); loving God,

We receive your gentle, powerful, healing touch.

For groups of people who are viciously scapegoated as the cause of the spread of AIDS, and too often pronounced "non-innocent" sufferers of AIDS diseases because they are poor, or black, or Puerto Rican, or gay . . . (silent prayer); loving God,

We receive your gentle, powerful, healing touch.

For families of someone dying of AIDS that are torn apart and divided because of ignorance and prejudice, or that are rendered entirely invisible, not recognized as a "real family" . . . (silent prayer); loving God,

We receive your gentle, powerful, healing touch.

For people stricken by grief at the death of a loved one from AIDS . . . (silent prayer); loving God,

We receive your gentle, powerful, healing touch.

For the sickness of indifference that infuses the fabric of our wealthy nation, tolerating a national policy that refuses to recognize the AIDS crisis that exists right *now* . . . (silent prayer); loving God,

We receive your gentle, powerful, healing touch.

For people with AIDS who suffer the daily insults of scorn, rejection, neglect, isolation . . . (silent prayer); loving God,

We receive your gentle, powerful, healing touch.

For national populations with people dying of AIDS in massive numbers, in countries such as Uganda, Tanzania, Zaire . . . (silent prayer); loving God,

We receive your gentle, powerful, healing touch.

Amen.

So be it.

Amen.

We are the church alive

6.6.8.6.8.6.8.6.

CHURCH ALIVE

TEXT: Jack Hoggatt-St. John & David Pelletier, 1980
MUSIC: Jack Hoggatt-St. John, 1980
Copyright © 1980 by the authors. Used by permission.

The Hymnal Project, © 1989 MCC San Francisco

STUDY QUESTIONS

Chapter 1: We Have AIDS

If you were preparing a sermon or meditation about AIDS to share with the members of your church, what Bible passages would you use for guidance?

Ron speaks of "learning to live in joy." Think of a time in your life when you were able to transform a difficult situation into a more positive one, and share this with your neighbor. What enabled you to do this (friends, church, scripture, and so on)?

Chapter 2: Letters to Connie

If you received a letter from someone in your family telling you she or he had AIDS, how do you think the church could be most helpful to you? Would you feel free to tell your pastor and others in the church? Why or why not?

Ron says, "We never can predict how our lives impact on others" (letter dated June, 1988). If you found you had AIDS, how could you have an effect on others, especially those in the church?

Chapter 3: A Journey Toward Freedom

John suggests that if the church was to become involved in ministry concerning the AIDS crisis, it might receive more than it gave. Has this happened to you or your church in other outreach ministries? Describe the process. What Bible passages come to mind as you discuss this?

A community of support or a faith community plays a vital role in the lives of persons living with AIDS. How has your faith community been helpful to you, and how has it been helpful to others?

Chapter 4: Space for Hospitality and Hope

What experiences have you had in which you felt "outside the gate"? In your understanding of church, are there some persons or groups who belong "outside the gate"? Why or why not?

The hymn texts used in the service seemed very important to the writer. If there are hymn texts that have special meaning for you, share them with the group. Perhaps a particular biblical text has been meaningful as well; share that also, if you wish.

Chapter 5: Dualism in Christian Tradition

The experience of AIDS has yielded valuable teaching moments, particularly when we "accompany" those who suffer on their pilgrimage of acceptance. Frequently this acceptance only is achieved through a pilgrimage of faith toward a more holistic and integrated sense of self-understanding.

In what ways do we die to our old self and rise to a new and strengthened attitude toward our situations in life?

How does our image of the church as an authentic healing presence challenge our presuppositions?

Chapter 6: Oppression and Resurrection Faith

Think of examples you have encountered recently in the newspaper, or in your own community, that demonstrate oppression. Can you think of examples that demonstrate oppression toward homosexual people (gays or lesbians)? What can your church do to proclaim a "resurrection faith" specifically for them?

What is the sin of which you (and your church) are guilty in relating to members of the gay community?

Chapter 7: Holiness and a Renewed Church

Suchocki takes up John's (chapter 3) suggestion that the churches become involved in the struggle with AIDS. She uses the first mark of the church, holiness, to make the case for such involvement. How does your understanding of holiness compare with hers, and do you reach similar conclusions?

By what procedures does your church seek to grow in holiness by engaging in actions of love for your congregation, for your community, and for the world?

Chapter 8: Marks of the Church in Times of Transformation

How has your church's self-understanding in the light of the marks of the church been altered by the AIDS crisis?

In what way is the AIDS crisis a healing for the divisions in the church?

Chapter 9: A Church for Troubled Waters

If you had not read the discussion of the marks and signs of the church in the chapters by Suchocki, Schreiter, and Russell, what would you have considered to be the characteristics of the true church?

The mark of justice is a necessity in Letty Russell's view of the church. Do you agree? Is the work toward justice for all creation a visible mark or sign of your own church? Would outsiders agree? What examples can you think of to illustrate a "justice church"?

Chapter 10: Life Stories

At what point in the life stories does the AIDS virus or how it is acquired become secondary? Why?

Why is acceptance of PWAs (compared with that of persons with polio, for example) a struggle for your church, and what does this say about your understanding of church?

Chapter 11: We Are the Church Alive

"Eschatological living" aptly describes how a greater sense of the responsibility to be agents of reconciliation has emerged when confronted with the struggles of the AIDS crisis. The ministry of the Metropolitan Community Church of San Francisco signals how expressions of reconciliation can bring new life. How has the AIDS crisis prompted a deeper awareness of the task of reconciliation both within and among churches, families, and friends in other areas of pain and struggle?

How do persons suffering with AIDS become teachers and witnesses of "faith coming alive" as a source of comfort and new hope?

Chapter 12: Who Is My Neighbor?

Sakenfeld asserts that the questions many of us raise about this text are not the questions Jesus is interested in. What do you suppose are some of the reasons we would rather discuss these side issues than engage ourselves in the heart of the story?

In what ways might your study group or your church help make the Jericho road safer? What might you do to respond as individuals and as a group to the AIDS crisis in light of your reflections on the Bible study? How does this Gospel story call you to respond?

Notes

Preface

1. *Minutes of the Meeting of the Standing Commission, 1984 Crete,* Faith and Order Paper No. 121 (Geneva: World Council of Churches, Commission on Faith and Order, 1984), pp. 33–42.

2. "Study on the Unity of the Church and the Renewal of Human Community: Working Group Process: 1985–1987" (New York: National Council of Churches, Commission on Faith and Order, March 1988; mimeographed).

3. Ibid.

Introduction

1. Where possible, scriptural quotations follow the Revised Standard Version of the Bible as found in *An Inclusive-Language Lectionary,* rev. ed., Years A, B, and C (Atlanta, New York, Philadelphia: John Knox Press, Pilgrim Press, Westminster Press, 1986, 1987, 1988). When the quotation is not found in these volumes, it will be quoted from the Revised Standard Version with any changed words in brackets. Any other version used will be cited in the text.

2. Julia Esquivel, *Threatened with Resurrection* (Elgin, Ill.: The Brethren Press, 1982), p. 61.

3. Ibid., pp. 65–66.

4.   *Women's Health Services Quarterly*, New Haven, CT 06511, Fall 1989, p. 1.

5.   Virginia Morris, "Yale battles AIDS dilemma," *New Haven Register* (Sept. 10, 1989).

6.   Numbers in brackets indicate a cross-reference to material found in this book.

7.   John A. T. Robinson, *On Being the Church in the World* (Philadelphia: Westminster Press, 1962), p. 132.

8.   The full denominational name is Universal Fellowship of Metropolitan Community Churches. In this book the abbreviations MCC and UFMCC both refer to the same denomination.

9.   Jennie Boyd Bull, "AIDS, Homophobia, and the Church: A Case Study from Metropolitan Community Church," in "Study on the Unity of the Church and the Renewal of Human Community: Working Group Report," National Council of Churches, March 1988, p. 3 (mimeographed).

10.   Michael Kinnamon, *Truth and Community: Diversity and Its Limits in the Ecumenical Movement* (Grand Rapids: Wm. B. Eerdmans Publishing Co., 1988), p. 17.

11.   Mary Catherine Bateson and Richard Goldsby, *Thinking AIDS* (Reading, Mass.: Addison-Wesley Publishing Co., 1988), p. 10.

12.   Adrienne Rich, "Natural Resources," *The Dream of a Common Language: Poems 1974–1977* (New York: W. W. Norton & Co., 1978), p. 57.

Chapter 1. We Have AIDS

1.   Cecile de Sweemer, "AIDS: The Global Crisis," in *AIDS Issues: Confronting the Challenge*, ed. David G. Hallman (New York: Pilgrim Press, 1989), p. 31.

2.   Kevin Gordon, "The Sexual Bankruptcy of the Christian Traditions: A Perspective of Radical Suspicion and of Fundamental Trust," in ibid., pp. 197–198.

3.   Peter Berger, *A Rumor of Angels* (Garden City, N.Y.: Doubleday & Co., Anchor Books, 1969), pp. 71–72.

4.   "Report from 'Illness and Health Stream,' " in Hallman, ed., *AIDS Issues: Confronting the Challenge*, pp. 157–158.

Chapter 4. Space for Hospitality and Hope

1.   Elisha A. Hoffman, "Leaning on the Everlasting Arms," *The United Methodist Hymnal* (Nashville: United Methodist Publishing House, 1989), No. 133.

2.   Paul Tillich, *The Shaking of the Foundations* (New York: Charles Scribner's Sons, 1948), p. 162.

3.   Lanny Wolfe, "Surely the Presence of the Lord," *The United Methodist Hymnal* (Nashville: United Methodist Publishing House, 1989), No. 328.

4.   Robert J. Dufford, "Be Not Afraid," *Glory and Praise* (Phoenix, Ariz.: North American Liturgy Resources, 1984), p. 26.

Chapter 5. Dualism in Christian Tradition

1.   Hans Küng, *Theology for the Third Millennium: An Ecumenical View*, trans. Peter Heinegg (New York: Doubleday & Co., 1988).

2.   Galatians was most likely constructed from a theological statement prepared by Paul at Antioch after the argument with Peter and then modified for sending to Galatia. This document would begin at 2:15 and might have concluded at 6:5. When the portions addressed to the Galatians in this section are removed, the theological argument flows with great clarity.

3.   Matthew Fox, *Original Blessing: A Primer in Creation Spirituality* (Santa Fe, N. Mex.: Bear & Co., 1983), and Gerald G. May, *Will and Spirit: A Contemplative Psychology* (San Francisco: Harper & Row, 1982).

4.   Though the relationship of Word/Wisdom in the Prologue, John 1:1–18, is clear, this is ignored in the rest of the

Gospel and even in 1 John 1:1–4, which comments on the Prologue. Love in 1 John is only love for the "brother" and not for the outsider. In the book of Revelation one encounters an enclave-like Christianity exhorted to stay pure from the world until God destroys all but the faithful.

5.   Though Paul uses the language of those given mercy and those condemned to destruction, he turns this language on its head, concluding in Romans 11 that "God has consigned all [people] to disobedience, that [God] may have mercy upon all."

6.   This is the implication of the way Matthew has cast the Sermon on the Mount (especially chapter 5) and the Great Commission in Matt. 28:18–20.

7.   Luke 15. This is part of a complex of three parables that move climactically toward the story of the father and his two children, all told in response to the accusation that Jesus associated with sinners and tax collectors.

Chapter 6. Oppression and Resurrection Faith

1.   In the following paragraphs, I am indebted to Suzanne Pharr's analysis of oppression in *Homophobia: A Weapon of Sexism* (Inverness, Calif.: Chardon Press, 1988), pp. 53–64.

2.   Ibid., p. 53.

3.   Randy Shilts, *And the Band Played On: Politics, People, and the AIDS Epidemic* (New York: St. Martin's Press, 1987).

4.   "A Hero Comes to Town," *Our Paper* (Portland, Maine), vol. 6, no. 5 (Jan. 1989), pp. 10–11.

5.   Aruna Gnanadason, "Women's Oppression: A Sinful Situation," in *With Passion and Compassion*, ed. Virginia Fabella, M.M., and Mercy Amba Oduyoye (Maryknoll, N.Y.: Orbis Books, 1988), p. 73.

Part Three: Signs of the Church

1.   "The Unity of the Church and the Renewal of Human

Community" (Geneva: World Council of Churches, Faith and Order Commission, 1989), FO/89:6 (mimeographed).

2. Cf. Jennie Boyd Bull, Introduction, note 9.

3. An example of convergence discussion is the Faith and Order report *Baptism, Eucharist, and Ministry* (Geneva: World Council of Churches, 1982). See also Michael Kinnamon, Introduction, note 10.

Chapter 7. Holiness and a Renewed Church

1. John Wesley, *A Plain Account of Christian Perfection* (1777; London: Epworth Press, 1979); henceforth referred to in text as CP.

Chapter 8. Marks of the Church in Times of Transformation

1. For the early history, see for example E. Dublanchy, "Église," in *Dictionnaire de Théologie Catholique*, 4:2128–2132. For a modern Roman Catholic view, see Gustave Thils, *Les Notes de l'Église dans l'apologétique catholique depuis la réforme* (Gembloux: J. Duculot, 1937). For a Protestant view, see Peter Steinacker, *Die Kennzeichen der Kirche* (Berlin: W. de Gruyter, 1982).

2. G. Limouris, ed., *Church, Kingdom, World: The Church as Mystery and Prophetic Sign* (Geneva: World Council of Churches, 1986), pp. 176–185, does this.

3. See Introduction, note 9.

4. For fuller accounts, see Steinacker, *Die Kennzeichen der Kirche,* and Yves Congar, "Die Wesenseigenschaften der Kirche," in *Mysterium Salutis* , ed. J. Feiner and M. Löhrer (Einsiedeln: Benziger, 1972), IV/1, 357–599.

5. Prompted by Letty Russell's 1987 Paul Wattson Lecture, "Unity and Renewal in Feminist Perspective." Lecture sponsored by the Franciscan Friars of the Atonement and the University of San Francisco and delivered at the university on January 23, 1987 (mimeographed).

Chapter 9. A Church for Troubled Waters

1. Cf. Cain Hope Felder, *Troubling Biblical Waters: Race, Class, and Family* (Maryknoll, N.Y.: Orbis Books, 1989). Felder draws his metaphor from the words of the African-American spiritual "Wade in the water: . . . God's a gonna trouble the water"; see p. xii.

2. Glenda Hope and Penny Sarvis, "Transformation in the Tenderloin," *Church and Society*, vol. 74, no. 3 (Jan.–Feb. 1989), pp. 45–50.

3. *AIDS Issues: Confronting the Challenge*, ed. David G. Hallman (New York: Pilgrim Press, 1989), p. xvii.

4. Cf. Bateson and Goldsby, Introduction, note 11.

5. Hans Küng, *The Church* (New York: Sheed & Ward, 1968), p. 268.

6. Jürgen Moltmann, *The Church in the Power of the Spirit* (New York: Harper & Row, 1977), p. 341.

7. John Calvin, "Preface," 1559 edition. Quoted in Hugh T. Kerr, ed., *Calvin's Institutes: A New Compend* (Louisville, Ky.: Westminster/John Knox Press, 1989), p. 11.

8. "The Scripture and Homosexuality," in John J. McNeill, *The Church and the Homosexual*, 3rd ed. (Boston: Beacon Press, 1988), pp. 36–66.

9. *Baptism, Eucharist and Ministry*, p. 2, cited in Part Three, note 3.

10. Ibid., p. 10.

11. Cf. James H. Cone, *Speaking the Truth: Ecumenism, Liberation, and Black Theology* (Grand Rapids: Wm. B. Eerdmans Publishing Co., 1986), p. 128.

12. Cf. Letty M. Russell, *Church in the Round: Ecclesiology in Feminist Perspective* (tentative title for forthcoming book [Louisville, Ky.: Westminster/John Knox Press]).

13. Alice Walker, "The Welcome Table," *In Love and in Trouble: Stories of Black Women* (New York: Harcourt Brace Jovanovich, 1974), pp. 81–87.

14. Küng, *The Church*, pp. 268–269.

15. Thomas F. Best, ed., *Living Today Towards Visible Unity* (Geneva: World Council of Churches Publications, Faith and Order Paper No. 142), pp. 14–15.

16. David T. Shannon and Gayraud S. Wilmore, eds., *Black Witness to the Apostolic Faith* (Grand Rapids: Wm. B. Eerdmans Publishing Co., 1988), p. 67.

17. James H. Cone, *For My People: Black Theology and the Black Church* (Maryknoll, N.Y.: Orbis Books, 1984), p. 123. Cf. also Jacqueline Grant, "Black Christology: Interpreting Aspects of the Apostolic Faith," in Shannon and Wilmore, eds., *Black Witness*, pp. 26–27.

18. Robin Scroggs, *Paul for a New Day* (Philadelphia: Fortress Press, 1977), p. 52. Cf. Kinnamon, *Truth and Community*, p. 37, cited in Introduction, note 10.

19. This was pointed out to me by Patricia Anderson, a student at Yale Divinity School in 1988.

Chapter 10. Life Stories

1. Rev. Donald Jackson, in the *Bay Area Reporter*, Sept. 29, 1988.

2. Ibid.

3. Anonymous, "Wearing the Scarlet Letter—AIDS," *The Baptist Standard*, vol. 99, no. 21 (May 27, 1987), p. 3. Used by permission.

Chapter 11. We Are the Church Alive

1. Adrienne Rich, "Natural Resources," *The Dream of a Common Language: Poems 1974–1977* (New York: W. W. Norton & Co., 1978), p. 57.

Chapter 13. Resources for Study and Action

1. Richard L. Schaper, "Pastoral Care for Persons with AIDS and for Their Families," *The Christian Century*, August 12–19, 1987, p. 691.

2. William E. Amos, Jr., *When AIDS Comes to Church* (Westminster Press, 1988), p. 55.

3. "An AIDS Primer," *Missions USA* (Jan.–Feb. 1989), p. 59.

4. "AIDS: A Challenge for Education and Action," *Light* (a publication of the Christian Life Commission, Southern Baptist Convention), March–April 1988, p. 3.

5. Ronald Sider, "AIDS: An Evangelical Perspective," *The Christian Century* (Jan. 6–13, 1988), p. 11.

6. Jane Parker Huber, "Creator God, Creating Still," from Huber, *A Singing Faith* (Philadelphia: Westminster Press, 1987), p. 9. Altered and used by permission of Westminster/John Knox Press.

J. Shannon Clarkson

Selected Bibliography

BOOKS

AIDS Project Los Angeles. *AIDS: A Self-Care Manual,* ed. Betty Clare Moffatt et al. Santa Monica, Calif.: IBS Press, 1987. A nontechnical treatment of the issues.

Alyson, Sasha, ed. *You Can Do Something About AIDS.* 1988. A public service project of the publishing industry, copyright 1988 by The Stop AIDS Project, Inc. Includes articles by celebrities, political figures, and caregiving professionals. Free from local bookstores.

Amos, William E., Jr. *When AIDS Comes to Church.* Philadelphia: Westminster Press, 1988. Written from personal experience to describe how a pastor and his church responded when AIDS entered their congregation.

Bateson, Mary Catherine, and Richard Goldsby. *Thinking AIDS: The Social Response to the Biological Threat.* Reading, Mass.: Addison-Wesley Publishing Co., 1988.

Blanchet, Kevin D. *AIDS: A Health Care Management Response.* Rockville, Md.: Aspen Publishers, 1988. An excellent volume covering health-care issues.

Callen, Michael, ed. *Surviving and Thriving with AIDS,* vol.

1: *Hints for the Newly Diagnosed.* New York: People with AIDS Coalition, 1987.

Church Education Services. *Breaking the Silence, Overcoming the Fear: Homophobia Education.* Ministries with Congregations, Program Agency, Presbyterian Church (U.S.A.). Available from Presbyterian Publishing House, 100 Witherspoon St., Louisville, KY 40203.

Crawford, Alma, et al. *Our Lives in the Balance: U.S. Women of Color and the AIDS Epidemic.* Kitchen Table: Women of Color Press, 1989.

Fee, Elizabeth, and Daniel M. Fox, eds. *AIDS: The Burdens of History.* Berkeley, Calif.: University of California Press, 1988.

Fortunato, John. *AIDS: The Spiritual Dilemma.* New York: Harper & Row, Perennial Library, 1987. Deals with the dilemma of the church, not the patient.

Griggs, John, ed. *AIDS: Public Policy Dimensions.* United Hospital Fund, 1987. An excellent, easy to read book on public policy.

Hallman, David G., ed. *AIDS Issues: Confronting the Challenge.* New York: Pilgrim Press, 1989.

Institute of Medicine/National Academy of Science. *Confronting AIDS: Update 1988.* Washington, D.C.: National Academy Press, 1988.

Jackson, Edgar N. *The Many Faces of Grief.* Nashville: Abingdon Press, 1977.

Kleinman, Arthur. *The Illness Narratives.* New York: Basic Books, 1988.

Kübler-Ross, Elisabeth. *AIDS: The Ultimate Challenge.* New York: Macmillan Publishing Co., 1987. Reflections on personal and professional work with persons with AIDS, including children.

Masters, William H., Virginia E. Johnson, and Robert E. Colodny. *Crisis: Heterosexual Behavior in the Age of AIDS.* New York: Grove Press, 1988.

Milliken, Weston, and Paul Stearns, eds. *Interfaith Confer-*

ence on AIDS and ARC. San Francisco: Interfaith Conference Steering Committee, 1987.

Moffatt, P. C. *When Someone You Love Has AIDS: A Book of Hope for Family and Friends.* Santa Monica, Calif.: IBS Press, 1986.

Nungesser, L. G. *Epidemic of Courage: Facing AIDS in America.* New York: St. Martin's Press, 1986.

O'Connor, Tom. *Living with AIDS: Reaching Out.* San Francisco: Corwin Publishers, 1986.

Pan American Health Organization. *AIDS: Profile of an Epidemic.* Scientific Publication No. 514. Washington, D.C., 1989.

Panem, Sandra. *AIDS Bureacracy.* Cambridge, Mass.: Harvard University Press, 1988.

Panos Institute Staff and Renee Sabatier. *AIDS and the Third World.* Philadelphia: New Society Publishers, 1989.

Peavey, Fran. *A Shallow Pool of Time: One Woman Grapples with the AIDS Epidemic.* San Francisco: Crabgrass Publishers, 1989.

Proceedings of the First International Conference. *The Global Impact of AIDS,* ed. Alan F. Fleming et al. New York: Alan R. Liss, 1988.

Ralston, Alissa. *What Do Our Children Need to Know About AIDS? Guidelines for Parents.* AIDS Interfaith of Marin County, 1000 Sir Francis Drake Blvd., No. 12, San Anselmo, CA 94960. Written by a professional AIDS/HIV educator and mother of three. Offers parents insightful and sensitive approaches to discussing difficult AIDS-related subjects with their children and teenagers.

Ruskin, Cindy, and Matt Herron. *The Quilt: Stories from the Names Project.* New York: Simon & Schuster, Pocket Books, 1988. Pictures and stories of quilt panels made by families, partners, and friends in memory of those who have died of AIDS.

Shafer, Margaret. *AIDS Bibliography: Selected Resources for*

Church Educators (January 1989). Division of Education and Ministry, National Council of Churches, 475 Riverside Dr., Room 705, New York, NY 10115.

Shelp, Earl E., and Ronald H. Sunderland. *AIDS and the Church.* Philadelphia: Westminster Press, 1987.

Shilts, Randy. *And the Band Played On: Politics, People, and the AIDS Epidemic.* New York: St. Martin's Press, 1987. Critically acclaimed behind-the-scenes political history of the AIDS epidemic in the United States.

Siegel, Bernie. *Love, Medicine and Miracles.* New York: Harper & Row, 1986. A surgeon discusses the role the spirit plays in healing.

Sontag, Susan. *AIDS and Its Metaphors.* New York: Farrar, Straus & Giroux, 1989.

———. *Illness as Metaphor.* New York: Farrar, Straus & Giroux, 1978.

Sunderland, Ronald H., and Earl E. Shelp. *AIDS, a Manual for Pastoral Care.* Philadelphia: Westminster Press, 1987. Focuses on pastoral-care dynamics for persons and families directly affected by AIDS. A how-to manual that is an excellent resource for deacons, laypersons, and clergy.

Switzer, David. *The Dynamics of Grief.* Nashville: Abingdon Press, 1970.

U.S. Department of Health and Human Services. *Surgeon General's Report on Acquired Immune Deficiency Syndrome* (Oct. 1986). P.O. Box 14252, Washington, D.C. 20044. Concise, comprehensive, factual presentation of information including transmission, prevention, and public health issues in C. Everett Koop's straightforward style. National resource directory included.

ARTICLES

"AIDS and A-Bomb Disease," by Chris Glaser. *Christianity and Crisis,* Sept. 28, 1987: 311–314.

Christianity and Crisis. July 4, 1988; entire issue deals with AIDS.

"Facing AIDS: Three Duties," by Gail Hovey. *Christianity and Crisis,* Feb. 15, 1988: 27–28.

"Houston's Clergy Consultation on AIDS," by Earl Shelp and Ron Sunderland. *Christianity and Crisis,* March 2, 1987: 64–66.

"Pastoral Care for Persons with AIDS and for Their Families," by Richard L. Schaper. *The Christian Century,* Aug. 12–19, 1987: 691–694.

"The Spiritual Challenge," by Edmond L. Browning. *One World,* Dec. 1987: 9.

"We Are the Church Alive, the Church with AIDS," by Kittredge Cherry and James Mitulski. *The Christian Century,* Jan. 27, 1988.

VIDEOS

A Letter from Brian. 29 min. For teenagers. Video, parent brochure, student workbook, and teacher/leader guide are available through local chapters of the American Red Cross.

Don't Forget Sherrie. 28 min. For black teenagers. Available through local chapters of the American Red Cross.

Talking with Teens. 27 min. For parents. Excellent resource. Includes vignettes of parents discussing AIDS with young people in informal settings. Very helpful for parents and sensitive to different parenting and cultural styles. San Francisco AIDS Foundation, P.O. Box 6182, San Francisco, CA 94101.

Too Little, Too Late. 48 min. 1987. Available from Greenwich Department of Health, 101 Field Point Rd., Greenwich, CT 06836. A documentary about the families of people with AIDS.

Women and AIDS: A Survival Kit. 22 min. For adult women. California AIDS Clearinghouse, University of California

Extension Media Center, 2176 Shattuck Ave., Berkeley, CA 94704.

RESOURCE PACKETS

AIDS: A Resource Packet for Congregations. National Council of Churches AIDS Task Force, Division of Church and Society, 475 Riverside Dr., New York, NY 10115.

JOURNALS

AIDS and Public Policy Journal. University Publishing Group, Inc., 107 E. Church St., Frederick, MD 21701. Published six times a year.

AIDS Literature and News Review. University Publishing Group, Inc., 107 E. Church St., Frederick, MD 21701. Published monthly.

Alert Newsletter. UFMCC, 5300 Santa Monica Blvd., Suite 304, Los Angeles, CA 90029. Published monthly.

Jubilee Journal: Social Concerns and the Episcopal Church. The Episcopal Church Center, 815 Second Ave., New York, NY 10017. Summer 1989.

DENOMINATIONAL POLICY STATEMENTS

Presbyterian Church (U.S.A.), Synod of the Northeast. Resolution on AIDS. Passed June 22–24, 1988, Potsdam, New York.

Progressive National Baptist Convention, Inc. Resolution on AIDS. Passed August 6, 1987, Houston, Texas.

United Church of Christ, General Synod 16. "A Pronouncement: Health and Wholeness in the Midst of a Pandemic." Passed June 25–July 2, 1987, Cleveland, Ohio.

NATIONAL ORGANIZATIONS

AIDS National Interfaith Network, 132 West 31st St., 17th Floor, New York, NY 10001.

Mothers of AIDS Patients, P.O. Box 89049, San Diego, CA 92138, Attn.: Barbara Peabody and Miriam Thompson.

National AIDS Network, 1012 14th St. NW, Suite 601, Washington, DC 20005. Resource organization providing technical assistance for community-based AIDS organizations nationwide.

National Association of People with AIDS (NAPWA), 2025 I St. NW, Suite 415, Washington, DC 20006.

National Minority AIDS Council (NMAC), P.O. Box 28574, Washington, DC 20003.

San Francisco AIDS Foundation, 333 Valencia St., 4th Floor, San Francisco, CA 94103. Catalog of educational materials available.

Women's AIDS Network, c/o San Francisco AIDS Foundation, 333 Valencia St., 4th Floor, San Francisco, CA 94103.